T0361292

Cambridge Elements

Elements in Corpus Linguistics
edited by
Susan Hunston
University of Birmingham

NATURAL LANGUAGE PROCESSING FOR CORPUS LINGUISTICS

Jonathan Dunn
University of Canterbury

CAMBRIDGE
UNIVERSITY PRESS

CAMBRIDGE
UNIVERSITY PRESS

University Printing House, Cambridge CB2 8BS, United Kingdom

One Liberty Plaza, 20th Floor, New York, NY 10006, USA

477 Williamstown Road, Port Melbourne, VIC 3207, Australia

314–321, 3rd Floor, Plot 3, Splendor Forum, Jasola District Centre,
New Delhi – 110025, India

103 Penang Road, #05–06/07, Visioncrest Commercial, Singapore 238467

Cambridge University Press is part of the University of Cambridge.

It furthers the University's mission by disseminating knowledge in the pursuit of
education, learning, and research at the highest international levels of excellence.

www.cambridge.org
Information on this title: www.cambridge.org/9781009074438
DOI: 10.1017/9781009070447

© Jonathan Dunn 2022

First published 2022

A catalogue record for this publication is available from the British Library.

ISBN 978-1-009-07443-8 Paperback
ISSN 2632-8097 (online)
ISSN 2632-8089 (print)

Additional resources for this publication at www.cambridge.org/dunnresources

Natural Language Processing for Corpus Linguistics

Elements in Corpus Linguistics

DOI: 10.1017/9781009070447
First published online: March 2022

Jonathan Dunn
University of Canterbury
Author for correspondence: Jonathan Dunn,
jonathan.dunn@canterbury.ac.nz

Abstract: Corpus analysis can be expanded and scaled up by incorporating computational methods from natural language processing. This Element shows how text classification and text similarity models can extend our ability to undertake corpus linguistics across very large corpora. These computational methods are becoming increasingly important as corpora grow too large for more traditional types of linguistic analysis. We draw on five case studies to show how and why to use computational methods, ranging from usage-based grammar to authorship analysis to using social media for corpus-based sociolinguistics. Each section is accompanied by an interactive code notebook that shows how to implement the analysis in Python. A stand-alone Python package is also available to help readers use these methods with their own data. Because large-scale analysis introduces new ethical problems, this Element pairs each new methodology with a discussion of potential ethical implications.

This Element also has a video abstract: www.cambridge.org/dunnabstract

Keywords: computational linguistics, natural language processing, corpus linguistics, text classification, text similarity, usage-based grammar, corpus-based sociolinguistics, computational stylistics, computational syntax

JEL classifications: A12, B34, C56, D78, E90

ISBNs: 9781009074438 (PB), 9781009070447 (OC)
ISSNs: 2632-8097 (online), 2632-8089 (print)

Contents

Accessing the Code Notebooks

https://doi.org/10.24433/CO.3402613.v1
https://github.com/jonathandunn/text_analytics
https://github.com/jonathandunn/corpus_analysis

To run the notebooks through Code Ocean, you will need to click the command that says "Edit Your Copy" in the top right-hand corner, as shown in the first screenshot:

The "Jupyter" command will now be available under the heading "Reproducible Run" as shown in the second screenshot:

This will start up the interactive notebook container. You can now find the notebooks within the "code" folder.

The following is a list of interactive notebooks together with the section of the Element which they accompany:

Lab 1.2. Accessing the Corpora

Lab 1.3. Visualizing Categories

Lab 1.4. Using Groupby to Explore Categories

Lab 1.5. Vectorizing Texts

Lab 2.1. Getting x and y Arrays for Dialects

Lab 2.2. Classifying Cities with TF-IDF and PMI

Lab 2.3. Classifying Authors with Function Word N-Grams

Lab 2.4. Using Positional Vectors for Parts of Speech

1 Computational Linguistic Analysis
1.1 Scaling Up Corpus Linguistics

Corpus linguistics has entered a golden age, driven by both the amount and the range of language that is now available for linguistic analysis. Corpus data is able to represent a population's usage at scale, bypassing the limitations which made introspection so important in the 1950s. But this wide availability of language data requires that linguists have the methods available to analyze it. And while there has been a surge of advances in natural language processing and computational linguistics, these advances have become increasingly disconnected from corpus linguistics and linguistic theory. This Element brings natural language processing and corpus linguistics together, showing how computational models can be used to answer both **categorization** and **comparison** problems. These computational models are presented using five case studies that will be introduced in the next section, ranging from syntactic analysis to register analysis to corpus-based sociolinguistics.

The goal here is to show how to use these computational models, what linguistic questions they can answer, and why it is important to scale up corpus linguistics in this way. A linguist can use this Element to learn how to use natural language processing to answer linguistic questions they are already familiar with. And a computer scientist can use this Element to learn about the linguistic assumptions and limitations behind computational methods, matters that are too often disregarded within natural language processing itself.

A categorization problem is about assigning a predefined label to some piece of language. At the word level, this could involve asking whether a particular open-class word is a noun or a verb. At the sentence level, this could be asking what kind of construction a particular sentence represents. At the document level, this could be asking whether a particular speaker represents New Zealand English or Australian English. All of these questions can be answered using a **text classifier**. This is a type of supervised machine learning in which we as linguists define the categories that we are interested in.

A comparison problem is about measuring the relationship between two observations. At the word level, this could be asking whether two nouns like *cat* and *dog* belong to the same semantic domain. At the sentence level, this could be asking whether two tweets have a similar sentiment. At the document level, this could be asking whether two articles are examples of a similar style. These questions can be approached using a **text similarity model**. This is a type of unsupervised machine learning in which we as linguists only control the representations being used, not the set of labels used for annotation.

How well do computational models compare with human introspection? In some cases, models can reproduce human intuitions with a high degree of accuracy. For example, text classifiers have been shown to make very good predictions about the part of speech of individual words when trained on small amounts of annotated data. In a case like this, a small amount of seed data, which is annotated by a linguist, supports the analysis of corpora too large to be annotated by a linguist. So a text classifier allows us to scale up introspection-based annotations.

In other cases, computational models can detect patterns in language that are not visible to human introspection. For example, research in both authorship analysis and dialect identification has shown that there are enough individual-specific and community-specific variants to enable accurate predictions of who produced a specific document. But, as linguists, our own introspections are not precise enough to identify these same patterns. In a case like this, computational linguistic analysis makes it possible to answer new questions about language.

Finally, there are cases where computational models completely miss something that is easily accessible to humans. For example, we will follow a case study on multilingualism online which shows that 90 percent of digital language data (from the web and social media) represents just twenty languages. Most languages in the world are low-resource languages from a computational perspective. As a result, many of the computational methods that we cover in this Element are difficult to apply to these languages. As linguists, however, we do not require millions or billions of words in a language before we can begin our analysis.

We need computational linguistic analysis for two reasons: for **reproducibility** and for **scalability**. First, every step in a computational pipeline is fully automated, which means that it can be reproduced and verified. For example, this Element follows five separate case studies that we will introduce in the next subsection. All the graphs and figures and experiments in the Element can be reproduced using the code notebooks that are linked within each section.[1] This is an example of how computational methods support reproducibility.

Second, the once-revolutionary Brown Corpus contained 1 million words (Francis & Kucera, 1967). But it is common now for corpora to range from 1 billion words, like the GeoWAC family of corpora (Dunn & Adams, 2020), up to 400 billion words, like the Corpus of Global Language Use (Dunn, 2020). These very large corpora are often drawn from digital sources like the web, social media, Wikipedia, and news articles. While these sources of language data have tremendous potential for testing linguistic hypotheses on a

---

[1]　And at https://github.com/jonathandunn/corpus_analysis

large scale, working with them requires computational methods to scale up the analysis.

At the same time, the combination of large digital corpora and computational linguistic analysis creates new ethical issues. Given that these corpora contain data from large numbers of individuals, how do we maintain privacy? How do we determine ownership and control over both the data and the models that are derived from the data? How do we prevent models from perpetuating negative stereotypes that are contained in these corpora? We will consider a range of ethical questions like these as we cover the core computational methods.

This first section introduces the basic ideas behind both text classification models and text similarity models. But, before we look at the models themselves, we start by introducing five case studies that we will be following to show how these methods can be used for meaningful linguistic analysis.

1.2 The Case Studies

This Element uses case studies and interactive code notebooks to show you how to apply computational methods using Python as part of a meaningful linguistic analysis. This section introduces the case studies and, at the end of it, you will find a link to a code notebook that introduces the corpora we will be using. Every example, every result, every graph that we use is reproducible given these code notebooks. This availability of both the code and the data is an important part of best practices.

Corpus-Based Sociolinguistics. This case study takes a computational approach to social variation. More precisely, we model geographic variation using digital corpora. These examples use data from the web and social media to model lexical and grammatical variation across different cities and countries (Dunn, 2020). The goal is to find specific linguistic features that are in variation across different populations, as well as to evaluate the distinctiveness or uniqueness of each set of variants. This case study is corpus-based because variants are discovered in naturally occurring corpora rather than elicited through survey-based methods.

Corpus Stylistics. This case study takes a computational approach to forensic linguistics. Do different authors have a predictable style? We use published books from Project Gutenberg (Gerlach & Font-Clos, 2020) to model how authors maintain a unique style across multiple works. What are the best features to capture stylistic variation? How unique are specific authors? Are these authorship models robust or do they depend on a small number of highly predictive features? The goal of this case study is to look at individual variation from a computational perspective.

Usage-Based Grammar. This case study shows how computational models can be used to analyze syntax and semantics. How can we identify which part of speech a word belongs to? How do we find which phrases are collocations in order to treat them as a single unit? Can we extract constructions from a corpus? Is it possible to cluster open-class words into semantic domains by observing their patterns of usage? These examples are drawn from the other corpora as well as from the Universal Dependencies data (Zeman et al., 2021). The goal is to undertake syntactic and semantic analysis while using corpus-based observations instead of introspection.

Multilingualism Online. This case study uses computational methods to analyze underrepresented languages in digital environments. What languages are found online? Where are these languages being used and for what purposes? Which languages have sufficient data and resources to enable a computational linguistic analysis? Can we use computational methods on languages other than English? What are the relationships between different digital registers? In addition to language-mapping data from the earthLings.io project,[2] this case study uses data from Wikipedia,[3] social media, and the web to look at register variation across dozens of languages.

Socioeconomic Indicators. This case study provides examples of how computational methods can be used to answer questions outside of linguistics. For example, how do political and social issues change over time? These examples use data from newspaper articles (Parsons, 2019) and congressional speeches (Gentzkow, Shapiro, & Taddy, 2018) to examine political discourse from 1931 to 2016. This case study further works with customer sentiment in the text of hotel reviews (Li, 2012; McKenzie & Adams, 2018). The goal is to augment traditional survey-based research methods by analyzing large corpora. These questions are not a part of the traditional domain of linguistics. They instead represent new practical applications of corpus analysis.

Taken together, these case studies show how to apply computational methods to a range of problems from different areas of linguistics, using Python to undertake the analysis. You can follow these case studies using the provided code notebooks as well as the associated Python package *text_analytics*.[4] For example, you can use this package to take a closer look at implementation details or to carry out your own analysis of your own corpora. Check out Lab 1.2 to explore the corpora from our case studies, shown in Table 1. After opening the lab capsule through Code Ocean, you will need to run the environment by

---

[2] www.earthLings.io
[3] www.tensorflow.org/datasets/catalog/wikipedia
[4] https://github.com/jonathandunn/text_analytics

Table 1 List of primary corpora used for the case studies

Corpus Source	Labels	N. Words
Congressional Speeches, 1931–2016	Year, Party	841 million
NYT Lead Paragraphs, 1931–2016	Year	364 million
Project Gutenberg Books	Author	1.04 billion
Tweets, Web Pages	City or Country	836 million
Hotel Reviews	Rating	353 million

following the *Jupyter* link. The notebooks are then contained within the *code* folder.[5]

The remainder of this first section provides an overview of the main topics we will cover. Section 1.3 discusses categorization problems (like part-of-speech tagging) and Section 1.4 discusses comparison problems (like corpus similarity). Section 1.5 introduces one of the central ideas in computational linguistics, that we represent language in a high-dimensional vector space. Finally, Section 1.6 is our first discussion of the ethical implications of computational methods, beginning with the idea of data rights. Each of the four main sections will have a similar structure, ending with a discussion of the ethical implications created by the methods we have just presented.

1.3 Categorization Problems

The first kind of model that we will cover is a text classifier, which we use to solve categorization problems. We start this kind of analysis by deciding which categories are important. In other words, we create a complete classification system, in which each unit of language belongs to one or another category. For example, if we want to apply part-of-speech tags to a corpus, we need to start by defining all the word classes that are available.

Let's say we want to sort tweets by language, in order to build a corpus of social media texts. We first come up with examples of all the languages we are interested in. Some categories might be quite large (a majority class, like English) while others are quite small (a minority class, like Samoan).

Then we train a classifier to automate the labeling task. Labeling here means assigning each text to the correct category. If a tweet is written in Samoan, we want the classifier to label it as Samoan. The goal, of course, is to automate labeling so that we can analyze our categories across corpora containing

---

[5] Lab 1.2 –> https://doi.org/10.24433/CO.3402613.v1

millions or billions of words. Training here means that we show the classifier examples with their correct labels until the model is able to make accurate predictions on its own.

Let's break down the problem of text classification. First, we need to consider the span of language that we are analyzing. In this Element we will look at examples of classifying individual words (like parts of speech), entire documents (like news articles), and collections of documents (like different writings from a single person).

Second, we need to design a category system. Sometimes this category system is straightforward: for example, if we want to classify documents according to their language or dialect, those categories are already well established (for example, English as a language or New Zealand English as a dialect). But there are other cases where we need to invent a new category system. Let's say we want to classify news articles by topic: We might start with a few high-level topics like SPORTS or POLITICS. But after some experimentation we will most likely find other topics that we have overlooked.

Third, we need to choose our representation to focus on a particular part of the linguistic signal. If the goal is to classify parts of speech, then we care about the surrounding context, especially surrounding function words. But if the goal is to classify news articles by topic, then key terms are more important than local syntactic contexts. And function words will not be helpful for making predictions about the topic of a document. In this Element we introduce four types of representation that allow us to capture different parts of the linguistic signal.

Fourth, we need to train and then evaluate a classifier. Our basic approach is to divide a corpus into **development**, **training**, and **testing** sets so that we can evaluate the model's output labels on samples that it has not seen. This prediction-based evaluation is important for ensuring that the results are valid. This is especially true when the ultimate goal is to use the predictions themselves for further linguistic analysis.

Let's think for a moment about the different kinds of categories that we might be interested in for corpus analysis. These examples come from the case studies. Sometimes we have syntactic categories, like parts of speech: Is this word a noun or a verb? Other times we have semantic categories, like topic: Is this article about SPORTS or POLITICS? The sentiment of a document can be seen as a pragmatic category: Is this review implying a good or bad experience at a hotel? And, finally, sociolinguistic categories involve stylistics or authorship analysis: What dialect does this document represent?

The power of a text classifier is that it allows us to undertake annotation for very different types of linguistic analysis. But we need to make sure that our representations of language (i.e., our features) correspond with the kind of categories we are working with. And, just as important, we need to make sure our category systems are coherent. Most classifiers are exhaustive and discrete, which means that every sample needs to be a member of one and only one category. For example, an article cannot be about both SPORTS and POLITICS in this framework.

At its core, we as linguists define the classification problem by deciding in advance what the categories will be. Some category systems are scientifically valid: For example, we know that we can identify the dialect or native language of a document's author. But other category systems are not valid: For example, we could not know what social clubs the author belongs to or what their favorite food is. We must establish a good justification for the categories we propose because the classifier will simply replicate any bias that we create in our annotations.

Check out Lab 1.3 to visualize the category systems for some of the categorization problems we will be working with.[6]

1.4 Comparison Problems

The second family of methods that we will cover is text similarity models, which we use to solve comparison problems. The basic idea is to measure how similar two words or two texts are, and then use that similarity to cluster them into groups. Similarity models are not discrete like classifiers and they do not require annotations in advance. For example, let's say we can measure that Charles Dickens writes more like Anthony Trollope than Ernest Hemingway does. Then we undertake that analysis for every pair of writers in a corpus. Now we have a network of relationships between authors that we can cluster into groups of similar authors. The final output is similar to a text classifier (these clusters are categories), except that we as linguists have not defined the labels.

We need to start by thinking about the same questions we posed for designing a text classifier: What span of language are we analyzing (words, sentences, documents) and what part of the linguistic signal are we interested in? For example, we will use similarity models to measure the association between words using both association measures (such as Pointwise Mutual Information) and word embeddings (such as the Skip-Grams with Negative Sampling architecture in WORD2VEC). In this case, the question is about the similarity of a particular word form across an entire corpus. But we will also look at models

---

[6] Lab 1.3 –> https://doi.org/10.24433/CO.3402613.v1

of corpus similarity and document similarity, which work across much larger spans.

Document similarity, for example, is a method that would allow us to sort news articles into finer-grained categories than a text classifier would support. And, more importantly, we as linguists would not need to predefine an exhaustive set of possible topics. The challenge, of course, is that there is not always an explicit connection between specific terms in an article (*home brew*) and the topic (BEER). So our text similarity model needs to learn that there is a topic in the background that can show up across various terms like *fermenter* and *siphon* and *yeast*. You might search for an article about *how to start a home brew* when you actually need to find an article about *how to soak your grains*. From a linguistic perspective, this is a challenge of finding relationships within a larger semantic domain.

Part of text similarity is the relationship between two texts or two words in isolation. That means that we just compare selections from Dickens and Trollope on their own, without considering other nineteenth-century novelists. But sometimes we want to know the relationship between all the texts in a corpus: The whole web for a search engine, or all English novels for a study of authorship. When we do this, we need a single fixed point for comparison. For example, we could define the location of every city in the world using its angle and distance from Rome and its altitude. Then we use these three numbers to represent where each city is located. Some similarity models work in just this way: We pick a set of points in vector space and map our texts relative to those points. In other words, if every document is represented using the same features, using a table with the same columns, we can directly compare those documents. **Vector space** is a way of thinking about high-dimensional representations of language, an idea that we will look at more closely in the next section. Relationships in vector space should mirror the linguistic relationships we are interested in.

Texts can be similar to one another because they have similar structures (syntax), similar content (semantics), similar implications or sentiment (pragmatics), or because they represent similar authors (sociolinguistics). We all use search engines like DuckDuckGo that work on content-based similarity. But the idea of a comparison problem more generally is that we could also build a search engine that includes authorship (news articles by Canadian women) or sentiment (news articles that have a positive view of urban cycling). The point is that if we can represent a particular part of the linguistic signal, then we can measure similarity between different samples (where a *sample* can be either a word or a document or a corpus).

A similarity model can be used to cluster documents, but it can also be used to cluster words. In addition to this, think about a document as a sample that represents some underlying population: Corpora from New Zealand also represent users of New Zealand English. Thus, we can also use similarity models to cluster abstract objects like dialects: What varieties of English are the most similar, given documents from each variety? Later we will see how to work at all three levels (words, documents, corpora). These problems are actually related to one another: for example, we could start with word similarity to see that *home brew* and *beer* and *keg* and *yeast* are all words that occur in a single semantic script. Then, a model of document similarity would start out knowing which words are related.

Text similarity models do not require us as linguists to define discrete categories in advance. On the one hand, this means it is possible for the model to find categories that we have not considered. We might think of HOME BREW as a topic that includes *beer* and *yeast* but forget about *bottles* and *sanitization*. An unsupervised model is easier to get started with, because there is not the initial work of creating a category system. On the other hand, it is much harder in practice to get these models to work well. The basic problem is that, because we do not tell the model what we want to get as output, we might not like the output that we end up with. Check out Lab 1.4 to further explore the corpora for our case studies.[7]

1.5 Language in Vector Space

The idea behind vector space is that we can find a representation for language in which the relationship between vectors mirrors the linguistic relationships that we are interested in. For example, the vector representation for nouns like *cat* and *dog* should capture the many lexical semantic properties of those words. The first step is to convert language into numeric representations, **vectors**, before we input those vectors into either text classifiers or text similarity models.

The way we choose to vectorize language depends on what part of the linguistic signal we want to analyze. The simplest method is to represent words using their frequency. Let's see what this looks like, starting with the sentences in (1) to (3).

(1) My neighbor sang a song about tulips.
(2) My neighbor sang a song about my neighbor.
(3) My neighbor sang a song about my tulips.

---

[7] Lab 1.4 –> https://doi.org/10.24433/CO.3402613.v1

Our first step is to make a table, where each word is a column (up and down) and each sentence is a row (left to right). The vocabulary looks like this when we go in alphabetic order:

	a	about	my	neighbor	sang	song	tulips

Now we count how many times each word occurs in each sentence. The number in each cell thus represents the frequency of the word shown in the column header. This means that words are columns and sentences are rows. The first sentence has the word *neighbor* just one time; but the second sentence has it twice. This gives us a frequency vector for each sentence.

	a	about	my	neighbor	sang	song	tulips
(1)	1	1	1	1	1	1	1
(2)	1	1	2	2	1	1	0
(3)	1	1	2	1	1	1	1

This is a toy example because the vocabulary is quite small (only seven words). For actual models we might work with 10k to 50k words. This means that the vector has 10k to 50k dimensions or columns, because each word in the vocabulary has its own column. The larger our corpus, the larger our vector space becomes.

Now let's walk through the process step by step. Take a sentence like (4), shown in the table below. The columns are individual words and the sentence is a row. This is called a **one-hot encoding** because each vocabulary item has a fixed position in the vector. The number in each cell is again frequency.

(4) That hotel has great views of Paris.

	every	great	has	hotel	in	of	Paris	that	views
(4)	0	1	1	1	0	1	1	1	1

Now let's say we have two other sentences, in (5) and (6). These are shown below, together with the frequency vector for (4). We notice a few things here: First, we could measure the distance between these vectors using metrics like Euclidean distance or cosine distance (which we will do in Sections 3.3 and 3.5). Second, small changes in the vectors actually represent large changes in the semantics: (5) is about just one hotel but (6) is about every hotel, a much broader scope for the statement. You will notice that this kind of representation would not work well for capturing scope.

(5) That hotel in Paris has great views.
(6) Every hotel in Paris has great views.

	every	great	has	hotel	in	of	Paris	that	views
(4)	0	1	1	1	0	1	1	1	1
(5)	0	1	1	1	1	0	1	1	1
(6)	1	1	1	1	1	0	1	0	1

A full-scale model needs to transform every document in a corpus into a shared vector space. Consider our case study of congressional speeches. The full corpus contains 2.7 million speeches, not just a handful. That means we will need a larger number of vocabulary features to fit each speech into the same vector space. It turns out there are 841 million word tokens in our corpus of speeches. As we would expect, though, most word types within the corpus are actually quite rare. The frequency graph in Figure 1 shows the number of occurrences for each of these unique word types in log scale.

The number of tokens for each word type drops off quite quickly. This means that we have a lot of uncommon words, occurring in just one or two speeches. There are just over a million word types. But only 626k word types occur at least twice, and 414k at least three times. This graph is in log scale, so that we can compare word frequencies across different orders of magnitude. These rare words do not add much information about the relationship between speeches, because they appear in so few documents. For practical reasons, we often limit the number of words we use, choosing the top *n* most frequent words. Everything else is considered to be **out-of-vocabulary** and is either ignored or replaced with a generic token.

Check out Lab 1.5, where we carry out this process for the entire corpus of congressional speeches. Because each speech shares the same one-hot encoding

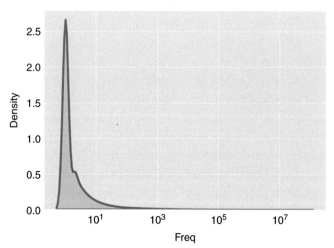

Figure 1 Distribution of word frequencies in congressional speech corpus

(where vector position *i* refers to vocabulary item *i*), we have converted each of the documents into the same vector space.[8]

1.6 Ethics: Data Rights

Computational models allow us to scale up our analysis to very large corpora. This allows linguists to analyze an amount of data that, as individuals, we could never hope to analyze. But it also creates some new problems. What happens when our ability to analyze very large corpora creates unintended applications? What happens when such data collection interferes with the privacy of individuals? If large corpora support profitable applications for corporations and governments, who should reap the rewards? Who controls language data? Who controls models that have been trained from language data?

Let's imagine that there is a new application of computational linguistics that derives knowledge about the world from a large corpus. And let's further imagine that this application is quite profitable. The basic situation is that average people create the data that makes such technology possible. But who benefits from that technology and who controls it? This is a relatively new area for human thought, and so our thinking about the ethics of such computational models has not caught up with the reality of how they are created and how they are used. As we explore how to use such models, however, we need to keep in mind that the analysis of large corpora can contribute to what has been called **surveillance capitalism** (Zuboff, 2019). How can we ensure that linguistic analysis is used only for specific ethical purposes?

A computational model only learns what we train it to learn. If the training data contains information that identifies individuals, the model inherits this breach of privacy. Here's a hypothetical example: Imagine we train an authorship model to verify that a bank customer who tries to access an account is actually the owner of that account. The bank which trains this model has millions of customers in the USA: mostly speakers from America, Canada, Mexico, and the UK. Other dialects, like New Zealand English, are used by only a handful of the bank's customers. How confident are we that the model remains accurate for a class of customers with very few samples? The model was trained and evaluated on distinguishing between millions of members from other classes. Do we trust that the model remains accurate for an unseen minority class? Could the model maintain information about individual members of that minority class?

---

[8] Lab 1.5 –> https://doi.org/10.24433/CO.3402613.v1

A model only knows what it finds in the data we train it with. So, if we train a model using data which implies that Klingons are violent, Romulans are lazy, Ferengi are drunks, and Vulcans are unintelligent, it is likely that the model will learn that these negative stereotypes are actual facts. Should we care whether our models are racist and xenophobic? Would such bias disqualify an otherwise accurate model? This problem is amplified in many cases because nonstereo-type information is never explicitly stated. In other words, even phrases like *a sober Ferengi* or *a peaceful Klingon* make reference to the underlying negative stereotype.

Minority groups are systematically disadvantaged by computational mod-els for two reasons: First, smaller groups have less privacy protection even in large data sets. This is because fewer training samples force generalizations to be made from fewer individuals. Second, most models require more data than is available for most languages. This means that populations which use non-majority languages are underrepresented. This raises an important question: Should groups like Indigenous people who are subject to special harm from these models have access to special protections from them? In other words, if the use of their data is more likely to harm Indigenous people, should they main-tain greater legal control over their data to prevent this from happening? This comes back to our initial questions: who controls the data? And who controls the models that depend on the data? Recent work has moved this conversa-tion beyond terms like *ownership*, which are insufficient to describe the overall problem.[9]

2 Text Classification

We will be looking more closely at text classifiers in this section. We start in Section 2.1 with a question about evaluation: How do we know when a text classifier actually works well? How do we have confidence in the models that we end up with? We then consider how to focus our vector space onto spe-cific parts of the linguistic signal: content or topic (Section 2.2), grammatical structure (Section 2.3), local syntactic context (Section 2.4), and pragmatic sen-timent (Section 2.5). Each of these sections focuses on a different vector space that is made up of different kinds of features. Once we have learned how to represent a corpus for classification, we discuss two important types of mod-els: logistic regression (Section 2.6) and feed-forward networks (Section 2.7). Finally, we end with a discussion of the ethical implications of implicit bias in text classifiers (Section 2.8).

---

[9] https://github.com/TeHikuMedia/Kaitiakitanga-License/blob/tumu/LICENSE.md

2.1 Evaluating Classifiers

Let's think about a problem from corpus-based sociolinguistics to put this into context. Our goal is to find the lexical and grammatical features that distinguish different dialects of English. For a corpus, we will use collections of tweets and web data from twelve different countries; these tweets provide examples of (digital) language use in these countries. These dialects come from all over the world, as you can see from the countries listed in Figure 2: from Australia to South Africa to Canada. We will see in later sections how to represent stylistic choices in a corpus. For now, assume we have a text classifier that uses syntactic features (in this case, construction frequencies) to predict whether a sample comes from Australia or New Zealand. How can we know whether these predictions are accurate?

First, we train a classifier by showing it examples of each dialect. We look at this in more detail in Section 2.6. Conceptually, we start by dividing our corpus into training data and testing data. Then, we show the classifier the training data: This is the part of the corpus that the classifier uses to distinguish between different dialects. But then we test the classifier on its predictions using the separate testing data. This part of the corpus is held-out: The classifier has never seen these samples. Let's say I have some test tweets in American English. What dialect does the classifier predict? If it predicts American English, that's good. But if it predicts New Zealand English, that's bad. And this is our basic approach to evaluation: We keep this separate testing data that our classifier never sees so that we can test the classifier's predictions.

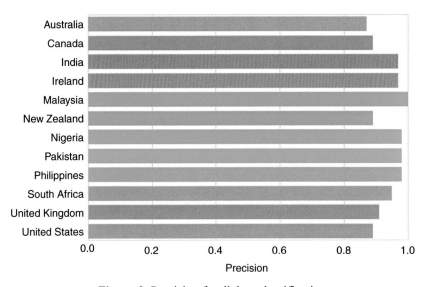

Figure 2 Precision for dialect classification

Table 2 True and false positives and negatives

	Predicted to be NZL	**Predicted to be** AUS
Correct	True Positives	True Negatives
Incorrect	False Positives	False Negatives

Let's think about New Zealand English. Suppose my classifier is trained to distinguish between just New Zealand English (NZL) and Australian English (AUS). First, we have some tweets from NZL that the classifier gets right. These are called true positives because the predictions are correct (true) and positive (NZL). This is shown in Table 2, with correct predictions in blue cells and incorrect predictions in red cells. Second, we have some tweets from Australian English that the classifier gets right. These are called true negatives because the predictions are correct (true) and negative (not NZL).

But what if the classifier is wrong? For example, we have some tweets in Australian English that our classifier predicts are from New Zealand. But we know they are from Australian English. These are called false positives because the predictions are false (incorrect) and positive (NZL). So the bottom left cell contains all the tweets from Australians that our classifier predicted to come from New Zealand. And finally we have false negatives: These are the tweets from New Zealand that the classifier thought came from Australia. So these four cells describe all the predictions that the classifier can make: true positives, false positives, true negatives, false negatives.

Now let's measure the quality of the classifier's predictions. The equation for a measure called **precision** is shown below. If the classifier identifies 100 tweets as New Zealand English but only 90 of those are actually from New Zealanders, the precision is 0.90. The higher the precision, the cleaner and more reliable the classifier's predictions. In other words, a high precision means that there are fewer false positives.

$$Precision = TP/(TP + FP) \tag{2.1}$$

Let's go back to our problem. Figure 2 shows precision for the twelve dialects in our classifier. The higher the precision, the fewer false positives there are. So these results show us that India is more precise than Australia. It is a more unique dialect. In other words, other dialects are not mistaken for Indian English.

The equation for another measure, **recall**, is shown below. If the classifier identifies 90 of the 100 tweets from New Zealand correctly, but gets 10 wrong

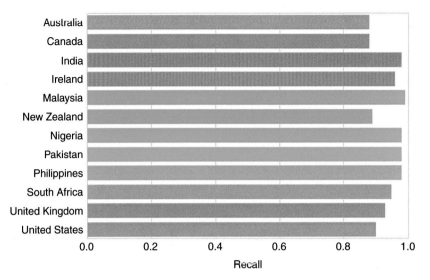

Figure 3 Recall for dialect classification

because it thinks they are from Australia, the recall is 0.90. The higher the recall, the more complete the collection of New Zealand tweets is. The lower the recall, the more New Zealand English the classifier has missed.

$$Recall = TP/(TP + FN) \tag{2.2}$$

Figure 3 shows the recall for our twelve countries. The higher the recall, the more likely the classifier has found all the examples of that dialect. You will notice that there are central dialects, like American and British English. These are harder to tell apart from other dialects because they have had a lot of influence. In other words, if British English is the mother of Nigerian English then it is going to look a little bit like Nigerian English. So the recall is a bit lower. On the other hand, look at Malaysian English. This is a unique dialect. Every time it sees Malaysian English, the classifier knows exactly what dialect it is. So recall is about measuring how complete our picture of each category is, and here the categories are national dialects.

Sometimes there is a gap between precision and recall. Look at Canada. The precision is not bad: 0.89. This means that a lot of what the classifier predicts to be Canadian English actually is. But the recall is just slightly lower: 0.88. This means that the classifier misses a bit more Canadian English, mislabeling it as some other dialect. If we look at the errors, it turns out that a lot of Canadian English is mistaken for American English. So even the classifier's errors tell us something about the categories that we are modeling. If we look at the errors for New Zealand, it is mostly confused with Australian English. And that also

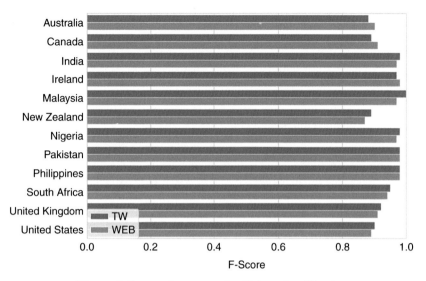

Figure 4 F-score by source for dialect classification

makes sense. So we have a classifier that is good at predicting what country a tweet is from based on syntactic features. And the errors that the classifier makes tell us which dialects are more similar. Models like this are the reason we can understand the styles of different writers using authorship analysis, something that we talk about later in this section.

But what if we want just one measure, instead of both precision and recall? The **f-score** is a variant of the average precision and recall. Basically, this takes both true positives and false negatives into account at the same time. Imagine that we have only 100 tweets from New Zealand and 1,000 from Australia. Then we could simply guess AUS every time and still end up with a precision of 0.91. In this case, though, the recall for New Zealand would be quite low. The f-score works well in cases of imbalanced categories, like when we have a lot more samples from Australia than from New Zealand. In other words, the f-score ends up a lot lower than precision in a case like this. And that is a more realistic measure of prediction accuracy.

$$F - Score = 2 * \frac{Precision * Recall}{Precision + Recall} \tag{2.3}$$

We show the f-score for each dialect in Figure 4. Here we have modeled the same national dialects from two independent sources of corpora: tweets and web pages. Both types of digital data provide an approximation of actual usage in a particular place. If the results for each dialect vary widely, this would indicate that one or both sources is a poor representation. What we see, instead, is that they largely agree in terms of the prediction accuracy for each dialect. In other words, this provides evidence for the robustness of this dialect model.

The main idea in this section is that, no matter what classifier we use, we evaluate it the same way: by testing its predictions on unseen samples. Precision tells us about the rate of true positives and recall tells us about the rate of false negatives. Finally, the f-score gives us a single measure of accuracy that also works well in cases where one category has a lot more samples than another. This section's lab[10] explores the use of constructions to represent syntactic variation. This is based on work in both computational construction grammar (Dunn, 2017, 2018b, 2019a; Dunn & Nini, 2021; Dunn & Tayyar Madabushi, 2021) and computational dialectology (Dunn, 2018a, 2019b, 2019c).

2.2 Representing Content

This section discusses in more detail how we can transform a document into a vector space that focuses on the semantic content of that document. You will remember that we start to represent the meaning of a document by counting the words it contains. Many types of corpus analysis are interested in the meaning or content of a text. What topic is this tweet about? What political issue does this speech discuss? When we talk about content in this way, the grammar and style and sentiment of the document are irrelevant. So we want to represent the content while ignoring these other parts of the linguistic signal.

In the previous section, we looked at the results of dialect classification, where the categorization problem was to determine the dialect region of the author of a document. We focused on how to evaluate the classifier, so we did not see how the model works in detail. Let's start by changing the problem: Instead of looking at syntactic representations, we will look at lexical representations. For this example, we take tweets from thirty different cities around the world. We want to learn what each city is like, what events are happening, what kind of people live there, what the human geography is. We can formulate this as a categorization problem: Can we train a text classifier to predict what city each sample is from using content words? This model will help us discover what makes each city unique, using the content of tweets.

To represent content, start by removing **stopwords** from the corpus. These stopwords include function words like *the* and *every* and *did*. They also include words, such as *seemed* or *going*, which have a grammaticalized meaning. The basic idea is that these words are so common across all documents that they do not contribute to the unique meaning of the documents; this is a view of

---

[10] Lab 2.1 –> https://doi.org/10.24433/CO.3402613.v1

meaning that focuses on the properties that distinguish one document from another. We might define the list of stopwords in advance, as we do in the *text_analytics* package. Or we could define the stopwords as the *n* most frequent words in the corpus. In (7a) we see an example sentence from the corpus and in (7b) we see that same sentence without stopwords.

(7a) Get or make an ebike and it'll pay for itself with extra benefits in no time

(7b) make ebike pay extra benefits

We then use the version of the sentence in (7b) to make a vector of content word frequencies. This vector ignores much of the linguistic structure to focus on the content of the sentence. Ultimately, we want to know what makes each of these cities different. Many topics will be equally common in every city: SPORTS, TRAFFIC, WEATHER. So we also use **Term Frequency-Inverted Document Frequency** (TF-IDF) to highlight distinctive words.

The idea is to adjust or weight the frequency of each word according to the number of documents it occurs in. For example, if *traffic* occurs in 100,000 tweets, then we want to reduce its overall importance. But if *blues* is rare in most cities, we want to increase its overall importance. Term frequency is what we have already been using: frequency alone, how many times a word occurs in a specific document. But the weighting term, inverted document frequency, represents the number of documents that the word occurs in. This is a measure of **dispersion**, capturing the degree to which words are equally spread throughout the corpus.

The word frequency in each document is weighted using the *idf* value. Weighting here just means that we make an adjustment to the raw frequency; thus, we are no longer using raw frequency alone. In the equation below, *df* is the number of documents (tweets) this word is observed in. And *n* is the total number of documents in the corpus. We add 1 to both values, in part to make sure that there are no values with 0. The final term, $+1$, ensures that each word is represented by at least its document frequency. For example, if *the* is found in every document, its idf will be 0. So the final term makes sure that common words are still accounted for. Finally, the logarithm allows the measure to accommodate different orders of magnitude for frequency values.

$$idf(word) = \log \frac{1+n}{1 + df(word)} + 1 \qquad (2.4)$$

Let's take a look at how this works. Let's say the word *the* occurs in 998 of 1,000 documents. But the word *blues* occurs in 14 of 1,000 documents. *n* is the number of documents in total (1,000). *df* is the number of documents that contain a word like *the* or *blues*. We add 1 to both terms, in part to avoid having 0 in either term. The core ratio is 1.002 for *the* and 66.73 for *blues*. Intuitively, this initial quantity is going to really highlight any occurrence of *blues*. And that is what we want, because it is rare and thus can be used to distinguish the documents which contain it. However, this version provides too strong an effect: 1 for *the* and 66 for *blues*. So we take the log and add 1. This smooths the measure and gives us a weight of 2.82 for *blues* and 1.008 for *the*. If we did not use the log to smooth these values, the weighting for rare terms would be too extreme.

So far we are representing content in vector space by removing stopwords, taking the frequency of the remaining words, and adjusting that frequency using TF-IDF to highlight words that occur in only a few documents. As we start to highlight less common words, we might notice some strange words: *angeles* or *katrina* or *erie*. The problem here is that we miss phrases with one common and one uncommon word. The actual features should be *los angeles* or *hurricane katrina* or *lake erie*. How can we learn which words are actually phrases that should be viewed as a single feature?

The answer has to do with probability: A phrase is when two words are almost as likely to occur together as they are to occur individually. We measure how strong the association of a phrase is using **Pointwise Mutual Information, or PMI** (Church & Hanks, 1990). Here we have the probability that *los angeles* occurs as a phrase over the probability of *los* on its own and the probability of *angeles* on its own. These probabilities become quite small, so we use the logarithm. The probabilities that we use here are actually just relative frequencies. In other words, the probability that w_1 and w_2 occur together is based on the frequency with which we observe them occurring together. In the labs, we use a normalized version of PMI, adjusted so that the values fall between -1 (words with no chance of occurring together) and 1 (words which always occur together).

$$PMI(w_1, w_2) = log\frac{P(w_1, w_2)}{P(w_1) * P(w_2)} \tag{2.5}$$

Here in Table 3 are some examples of the kinds of phrases that PMI gives us from the tweets. We have names of places like *Baton Rouge* and names of events like *Typhoon Hato*. Then we have names of people like *Rudy Giuliani* and names of organizations like *Hillbrow Radio*. And finally we get collocations: *herd immunity* and *sanitary napkins* and *chest pains*. We get these phrases before we do any other processing.

Let's review: We are looking at the frequency of words. But many function words do not reflect the content of a document, so we first remove stopwords. And frequency alone emphasizes common words, so we use TF-IDF weighting to

Table 3 Phrases using Pointwise Mutual Information

Places	*causeway bay, gallery in putney, southeast asia*
People	*coco chanel, duke of sutherland, ringo starr*
Terms	*sanitary napkins, herd immunity, chest pains*

Table 4 Classification results for thirty cities using tweets

	Precision	**Recall**	**F-Score**	**N. Test**
Adelaide	0.92	0.91	0.92	503
Atlanta	0.94	0.92	0.93	542
Auckland	0.98	0.99	0.99	479
Bengaluru	0.95	0.94	0.95	487
Boston	0.96	0.92	0.94	504
...	...	...	...	...
San Francisco	0.95	0.95	0.95	479
Seattle	0.95	0.96	0.95	492
Singapore	0.99	1.00	0.99	501
Sydney	0.84	0.84	0.84	457
Toronto	0.96	0.97	0.96	520
Washington	0.94	0.96	0.95	472
Weighted Average	**0.95**	**0.95**	**0.95**	**15,003**

highlight uncommon words. And rather than rely on individual words, we find multi-word expressions using PMI as a measure of association. Now we have represented the content of our tweets by converting them into a single shared vector space.

Here in Table 4 we are looking at precision, recall, and f-score by city for our problem of distinguishing between different cities using what we might call human geography. This is based on content, the opposite of the dialect classification that we looked at last time. We might also think about this as a model of lexical variation, except that we have not controlled for differences in topic. The predictions are quite good across 15,000 total test samples (each sample is an aggregation of tweets). The model can tell us a lot about the social and geographic characteristics of each city, beyond just the city label. The model captures the properties that make each city unique and that is why it can make such good predictions about the labels. In this section's lab, we reproduce these city classification results and explore them in a bit more detail.[11]

---

[11] Lab 2.2 –> https://doi.org/10.24433/CO.3402613.v1

2.3 Representing Structure

The linguistic signal also carries information about structure (syntax). This is information which we purposely covered up in the previous section. In the next section we will look at how to represent grammatical structure for the purpose of directly modeling syntax for part-of-speech tagging. But first let's use grammatical structure to model sociolinguistics: stylistic variation across individual authors. The case study focuses on authorship for nineteenth-century books: Can we determine who wrote a given selection from a book?

Look at the examples below in (8a) to (8e). Each of these examples has the same general meaning. And each example would have a very similar representation given our methods for representing content. But the syntax of each sentence is quite different.

(8a) I go around puddles when I bike to work.
(8b) I avoid puddles when biking to work.
(8c) I avoid puddles on my way to work.
(8d) I hate cycling through puddles on my commute.
(8e) Puddles are something I always go around when I am commuting.

We can use these grammatical differences to predict sociolinguistic information about the text's author: gender, dialect, native language, and sometimes even age and class. The basic idea is that we all (unconsciously) prefer different variants. A variant here is an alternation, like *go around* vs *avoid* or like *on the way to work* vs *commuting*. We have many choices like this in every sentence that we produce, tens of thousands of choices (Dunn, 2018a). How can we represent a corpus to focus on these kinds of grammatical choices?

In analytic languages like English, function words are a good proxy for grammatical structure. Function words are things like pronouns (*you, me*), conjunctions (*and, or*), prepositions (*in, on*), auxiliary verbs (*was, were*), and wh-words (*who, what*). But they also include common words with a grammaticalized meaning (such as *going* or *seem*). Of course, English syntax has a much richer structure than these features are able to pick up. But function words are easy to identify and count. That ease of use has made them a good first tool for representing grammatical structure in a corpus.

Stylistics offers a glimpse into demographics. In other words, one of the fundamental properties of language is that it encodes social attributes. From this perspective, each of us belong to different groups, different combinations of social attributes. Some of our linguistic patterns come from larger groups (dialects) and some of them are specific to us as individuals. In and of itself, each stylistic feature is meaningless. But, taken together, the structure of a text provides a pointer to the individual who produced it.

Table 5 Examples of function word n-grams

from the	were too	there is	must be
by way	through the	is very	away it
way of	with the	very little	it is
at that	we shall	in it	they know

We also use different language in different contexts. For example, people writing an email to someone in authority (like their boss) would say something like *I'm wondering if you have time for a meeting with me tomorrow?* But people writing an email to someone under their authority (like an employee) are more likely to say something such as *Let's meet tomorrow afternoon to discuss the report.* We can see that there are significant differences here in the use of pronouns and other function words (Pennebaker, 2011). This suggests that we can use function words as a proxy for these syntactic variations.

So far we have counted the frequency of individual words and phrases. From this perspective, the order of words in a sentence is irrelevant because a word's position in the vector is not related to its position in the sentence. But for syntactic structure this assumption no longer works. For example, *I am going to the store* and *Am I going to the store* have very different meanings. In other words, the choice of *I am* vs *am I* has a significant impact on the meaning. An **n-gram** is a way of counting words while retaining order. If we count pairs of two words we call these bigrams (like *I am*); and if we count sets of three words we call these trigrams (like *would have been*). When we use n-grams, we count each pair of words as if it were just one unit. Table 5 shows a few examples of sequences that are function word n-grams.

Let's see how the sentences in (8) look when we represent them using vectors of function words (focusing only on unigrams for the sake of space). The table below shows our vector space representation of the sentences, using only grammatical items as features. Even though the sentences have the same content, their syntactic vectors are quite different.

	always	am	are	around	I	my	on	through	to	when
(8a)	0	0	0	1	2	0	0	0	1	1
(8b)	0	0	0	0	1	0	0	0	1	1
(8c)	0	0	0	0	1	1	1	0	1	0
(8d)	0	0	0	0	1	1	1	1	0	0
(8e)	1	1	1	1	2	0	0	0	0	1

Let's model variation in these features using books from Project Gutenberg, looking at authors born between 1850 and 1900. We will be working with over

Table 6 Classification results for twenty-four authors Using published books

	Precision	Recall	F-Score	N. Test
Jane Abbott	0.98	0.99	0.99	102
Joseph Altsheler	1.00	1.00	1.00	59
Arnold Bennett	1.00	1.00	1.00	45
Harold Bindloss	1.00	1.00	1.00	80
Arthur Conan Doyle	1.00	1.00	1.00	68
...	...	...	...	...
Mrs. Humphry Ward	0.97	0.99	0.98	75
Charles Warner	1.00	0.91	0.95	23
Carolyn Wells	0.98	0.98	0.98	48
Stanley Weyman	1.00	0.98	0.99	51
Henry Wood	1.00	0.97	0.98	61
Weighted Average	**0.99**	**0.99**	**0.99**	**1,600**

1,100 books written by 24 different people (only those who wrote at least 4 different books). We first break up each book into a bunch of smaller parts, chapter-size chunks of about 5,000 words. The question is, how well can a text classifier predict who wrote each of these chapters, given a vector of function word n-grams?

Here in Table 6 are the results of our experiment. We train the classifier on one set of samples, then test it on another set. We will talk about how to train the classifier in a later section. For now, we see that a text classifier is very good at distinguishing between different authors. The overall f-score is 0.99. None of the content is represented here, so we know this has nothing to do with terms like *Sherlock Holmes*. This model only has access to function word n-grams that are a proxy for the syntactic choices made by different writers.

In this section's lab, we show how to recreate this experiment in authorship analysis with a bit more detail.[12]

2.4 Representing Context

In the previous section we represented syntactic choices throughout an entire document using function word n-grams. This tells us a great deal about the overall style of that document, but this kind of representation would not be

---

[12] Lab 2.3 –> https://doi.org/10.24433/CO.3402613.v1

Table 7 Universal parts of speech as a categorization system for words

Open Class	Closed Class	Other
ADJ (adjective)	ADP (adposition)	PUNCT (punctuation)
ADV (adverb)	AUX (auxiliary verb)	SYM (symbol)
INTJ (interjection)	CCONJ (co-ordinating conj)	X (other)
NOUN (noun)	DET (determiner)	
PROPN (proper noun)	NUM (numeral)	
VERB (verb)	PART (particle)	
	PRON (pronoun)	
	SCONJ (subordinating conj)	

helpful for a problem like predicting the part of speech of individual words. Here we will put together a **positional vector** which better represents the syntactic context for individual words. This is a better representation for making predictions about words because it captures the specific linguistic context of each particular token.

We start by coming up with a set of syntactic word classes, drawn from the Universal Part-of-Speech tag set (Petrov, Das, & McDonald, 2012). As shown in Table 7, there are two main categories: open-class words (like nouns and verbs) and closed-class words (like adpositions and pronouns). You will notice that there are also catch-all categories (like X or SYM). These are important because every word in a corpus needs to be tagged. If we are not sure what the syntactic class should be, these miscellaneous categories are helpful. In our previous categorization problems, we relied on nonlinguistic information for our categories (like New Zealand English as a dialect or Arthur Conan Doyle as a writer). Here we directly annotate linguistic categories, like noun and verb.

We represent each word given the surrounding context window. Consider the sentence in (9). For each word, we want to know the words which come before and after it. These context windows are shown in (9a) through (9c), with the target word in small caps and bold. Here we use a window size of two words before and after. Each word is thus represented by a sequence of five items, with the word itself in the center position.

(9) We are aware of six studies designed to investigate the question.

(9a) are aware **OF** six studies

(9b) aware of **SIX** studies designed

(9c) of six **STUDIES** designed to

We convert this sequence into a one-hot encoding of positions. A one-hot encoding, you will remember, is a vector in which each dimension represents a single piece of information. In the vector representation below, we represent just two positions: the first word (1) and the last word (5). So if the first word is *are*, as in (9a), the vector starts with a 1. But otherwise the vector starts with a 0. This positional vector represents each word within its immediate context.

	1=*are*	1=*aware*	1=*of*	5=*studies*	5=*designed*	5=*to*
(9a)	1	0	0	1	0	0
(9b)	0	1	0	0	1	0
(9c)	0	0	1	0	0	1

We use the training corpus to find the vocabulary and fit a one-hot encoding to represent the observed sequences of words. Of course, we will never observe all possible word sequences in the training corpus. We resolve this problem by having a special token that represents an **out-of-vocabulary** word. For example, consider the example in (9b'), where we have *studies* as a missing out-of-vocabulary word. In this case, the other parts of the context are still represented, giving the tagger a chance to still make a correct prediction.

(9b') are of SIX [OOV] designed

The larger our vocabulary and the longer the context we use for each word, the larger this positional vector will become. We will see in the labs how to easily convert sentences into this format; although it is not easy for linguists to interpret these vector representations (as opposed to frequency vectors, for example), they are not problematic for a text classifier.

We use a logistic regression classifier (see Section 2.6) to predict the part-of-speech tag for each word given a one-hot encoded positional vector. Some classes, like DET or ADP, should be easier to predict because they form a closed class. This is exactly what we find in the results in Table 8. The overall prediction quality achieves an f-score of 0.93 across nearly 56,000 word tokens. More advanced taggers have improved upon this level of performance. The point here, however, is to show how to use a positional vector to represent syntactic information; even this simple approach performs quite well on the task.

You will notice that the categories which lower the overall performance are those which serve as catch-all categories, for example X. This is because these categories contain precisely those tokens which are difficult for us to categorize

Table 8 Classification results for predicting parts of speech

	Precision	Recall	F-Score	N. Test
ADJ	0.89	0.84	0.87	3,698
ADP	0.93	0.97	0.95	5,334
ADV	0.90	0.80	0.85	2,540
AUX	0.95	0.97	0.96	3,032
CCONJ	0.99	0.99	0.99	1,801
DET	0.97	0.97	0.97	4,650
INTJ	0.97	0.77	0.86	181
NOUN	0.86	0.95	0.90	9,798
NUM	0.95	0.85	0.90	958
PART	0.95	0.97	0.96	1,420
PRON	0.96	0.96	0.96	4,575
PROPN	0.87	0.76	0.81	3,156
PUNCT	0.99	1.00	0.99	6,816
SCONJ	0.84	0.76	0.80	1,060
SYM	0.93	0.64	0.76	134
VERB	0.92	0.91	0.92	6,165
X	0.92	0.28	0.43	128
Weighted Avg	**0.93**	**0.93**	**0.93**	**55,947**

as linguists. We show how to create a positional vector to capture syntactic information in the lab for this section.[13]

2.5 Representing Sentiment

Now that we have represented content, structure, and context, the final part of the linguistic signal that we can use for text classification is sentiment (pragmatics): What is the tone or emotion expressed in the text? This is important because two similar authors might write about the same topic from very different perspectives. Look at the sentences in (10a) and (10b), where words that carry sentiment are shown in brackets. Both sentences have the same basic meaning, if we had used our content representation: There is a piece of legislation in congress that would let one branch of government carry out a new authority. But the opinion expressed in (10a) is negative while the opinion in (10b) is positive. This difference is what we mean by the term **sentiment analysis**.

---

[13] Lab 2.4 –> https://doi.org/10.24433/CO.3402613.v1

(10a) The [*awful*] amendment under consideration grants [*frivolous*] powers to the executive branch, [*threatening*] [*disastrous*] effects for many [*horrible*] years.

(10b) The [*well-crafted*] amendment under consideration grants [*vital*] powers to the executive branch, [*promising*] [*meritorious*] effects for many [*wonderful*] years.

If we represented these sentences using content words, they would look the same in vector space. If we looked at the form of these sentences, we would see exactly the same function word n-grams. The only difference between them is sentiment. We take a **dictionary-based** approach to sentiment (Wang, Lu, & Zhai, 2011): We have a list of positive words and a list of negative words. These positive and negative words, and nothing else, will provide our features when we convert texts into numeric vectors for sentiment analysis. Because the dictionary is defined in advance, by linguists, we do not need measures like TF-IDF or PMI to improve the representation.

In this Element we take a traditional approach to representing sentiment, which divides words into POSITIVE and NEGATIVE and NEUTRAL, where neutral words are not used for sentiment analysis. Thus, our dictionary creates a list of words which are considered to be POSITIVE or NEGATIVE regardless of their specific context. From a linguistic perspective, this is a simplifying assumption. We know that there are types of pragmatic meaning like metaphor, irony, sarcasm, and humor in which the context can radically change the meaning of a word (Dunn, 2013a, 2013b, 2014). And we know that there are more types of pragmatic meanings, like politeness and register, which might be considered alongside sentiment. Although this approach to representing sentiment ignores these finer distinctions, it remains effective for many problems.

Sentiment features are language-dependent. Content features, using TF-IDF and PMI, can be created for any language. And the equivalent of function word n-grams can be created by choosing the most frequent words to approximate function words. But we, as linguists, would need to annotate the sentiment lexicons for each new language, with the effect that sentiment representations are the most difficult to transfer across languages.

Let's say we wanted to understand tourist behavior in the aggregate using hotel reviews. Content analysis can tell us *what* is being talked about: hotels, restaurants, arts venues, sports venues, and so on. Authorship analysis can tell us *who* each reviewer is, the demographics of the people who produced the data. And now sentiment analysis can tell us *how* the reviewer enjoyed their experience.

Table 9 Vectors for sentiment analysis

POS	enjoyed	stylish	polite	courteous	always	appealing
(10a)	1	1	1	1	1	1
(10b)	0	0	0	0	0	0

NEG	endured	drab	rude	impersonal	never	nightmarish
(10a)	0	0	0	0	0	0
(10b)	1	1	1	1	1	1

Imagine two Americans visiting the same hotel; one hates it and the other one loves it. How do we know which is which? Think about these two sentences:

(11a) I [*enjoyed*] a [*stylish*] hotel room with [*polite*] and [*courteous*] staff [*always*] available in the [*appealing*] lobby.

(11b) I [*endured*] a [*drab*] hotel room with [*rude*] and [*impersonal*] staff [*never*] available in the [*nightmarish*] lobby.

The first sentence is from a positive review. The second is from a negative review. When we convert these into a vector space that represents sentiment, using our dictionary of positive and negative words, we get the vectors that we see in Table 9. We have separated the positive and negative words into two vectors to highlight how different the representations have become.

We already have a dictionary of positive and negative words, so we just count how many times each word occurs in each review. These examples are straightforward because the positive review has only positive words. And the negative review has only negative words. You will also notice that these sentiment words cross syntactic categories: verbs (*endured*), adjectives (*rude*), and even adverbs (*never*).

Now let's try this out on a real-world data set. We have about 2 million hotel reviews in the corpus and we want to use them to figure out which hotels are good and which ones are not so good. Since we want to know about hotels, we put all the reviews about one hotel together into a single document. This approach will tell us about the hotel itself rather than about individual reviewers. Next we train the classifier, so we need to find the average rating for each hotel to be our ground-truth label. This gives us a float between 1 and 5 for each hotel: the average rating. But a classifier needs discrete boxes. So we bin these reviews. In other words, we need to make that decimal number (float) into categories. We define everything below three stars as LOW and everything above four stars as HIGH.

Table 10 Classification results for hotels by Average Rating

	Precision	**Recall**	**F-Score**	**N.Test**
LOW Rating	0.99	1.00	1.00	363
HIGH Rating	0.99	0.99	0.99	167

The predictions, shown in Table 10, are quite good. That means the classifier has gotten almost every hotel correct. Looking at the number of samples, you can see we are making predictions about 530 different hotels that the classifier has never seen before. So that tells us the classifier has learned to generalize the features that distinguish between good and bad hotels. A linguistic analysis of sentiment is more nuanced, as we have already discussed. But, in cases like hotel reviews, a simpler approach works very well for applying corpus analysis to problems that are outside of linguistics itself. In the lab for this section, we show how to replicate this analysis of hotel reviews in Python.[14]

2.6 Logistic Regression

We have seen how to evaluate the predictions that a text classifier makes on held-out testing data, using precision and recall and the f-score. We have also seen how to represent language in vector space so that we highlight different parts of the linguistic signal. But we have not considered the inner workings of a text classifier or how we go about training a model. In the next two sections we will consider logistic regression and then feed-forward neural networks. These models convert a high-dimensional vector that represents the input (for example, function word frequencies) into a single value that represents the predicted class (for example, the author). The final part of this section will consider the ethical implications of implicit bias in text classifiers.

The basic idea for logistic regression is to learn a weight for each feature or dimension in our input vector. The goal of the classifier is to find the best feature weights ($w_1...w_n$) for distinguishing between our category labels. The difficult part of the task is to update these weights in order to find the model state which makes the best predictions. To figure out this problem, the classifier uses a **classification function** to make class predictions from the scalar output of the feature weights. And it uses an **objective function** to measure how many errors the current feature weights produce. These components are listed in Table 11.

---

[14] Lab 2.5 –> https://doi.org/10.24433/CO.3402613.v1

Table 11 Components of logistic regression

	General Type	Specific Name
1	Feature Weights and Bias	$w + b$
2	Classification Function	*Sigmoid*
3	Objective Function	*Cross-Entropy Loss*

This algorithm takes as input our feature vectors that represent each sample. Let's take as an example the problem of identifying how good a hotel is given a set of hotel reviews. For each hotel, x is our vector of sentiment word frequencies. And y is our ground truth, the quality of the hotel. Each feature in our input vector, x, has its own weight, w. Both the feature and the weight are scalar values: We might have a feature value of 1 and a feature weight of 0.1, as in the first position in the vector below.

$$x = [1, 4, 3, 0, 0, 1, 0, 2, 0, 3, 0, 2, 3] \tag{2.6}$$

$$y = \text{HIGH} \tag{2.7}$$

$$w = [0.1, 0.4, 0.3, 0.1, 0.4, 0.1, 0.1, 0.2, 0.1, 0.3, 0.1, 0.2, 0.3] \tag{2.8}$$

The notation below uses a **dot product** to indicate that each feature is multiplied by its own weight and the result is summed across all features. So, if the feature *awful* occurs 5 times and its current weight is 0.25, the result is $5 * 0.25 = 1.25$. This float (a scalar number) is added together with every other feature to produce a single float as output. In some cases, a fixed **bias** term is added, b, which would also be learned as part of the training process. The output of the dot product operation is a single float, z, which represents the classifier's current output for the current input sample.

$$z = w \cdot x + b \tag{2.9}$$

But this value, z is still not a prediction from a human perspective. Logistic regression is an example of binary classification because it works with only two classes. To make a prediction, the algorithm uses a classification function that takes z and converts it into a class prediction, y. In the case of logistic regression, the **sigmoid** is used as a classification function, shown below. You will remember that y is our label, in this case whether the hotel's average rating is HIGH or LOW.

The purpose of the classification function (here, the sigmoid) is to force the value of z (the combination of observed features and hypothesized feature weights) away from the dividing line. As shown in Figure 5, if the value of z

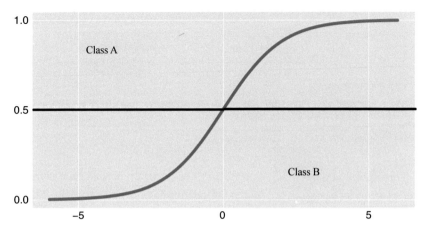

Figure 5 Relationship between z and y for the sigmoid

is below 0.5, the model predicts one class (HIGH). But if the value of z is above 0.5, the model predicts the other class (LOW). The effect of the sigmoid is to push values away from the middle point. The black horizontal line shows the threshold: Class A is any value above the line and Class B is any value below the line. This is how we convert the scalar value of the input weights to the discrete value of the output label.

$$y = \frac{1}{1 + e_{-z}} \tag{2.10}$$

This combination of feature weights and classification function allows logistic regression to make predictions. But how does the model learn the right feature weights? There are several training algorithms available, for example stochastic gradient descent. These algorithms optimize the feature weights by minimizing the amount of error produced by the model. The important point here is how we measure model error: Logistic regression uses the **binary cross-entropy loss** as an objective function, because it is dealing with just two classes.

When we evaluate the trained classifier, we use measures of accuracy (precision, recall, f-score). But we use a more specific optimization function during training because we want the model to make predictions that are far away from the dividing line. In other words, the prediction $z = 0.45$ for a negative sample would make a correct prediction, because it falls into the negative class. But a prediction $z = 0.10$ is a better prediction because it is further away from the dividing line. It is *more* correct. And cross-entropy loss provides a measure of the degree to which this second prediction is better.

Here's where we are: We extract a feature vector to represent each hotel review, x, and the model hypothesizes weights for each feature, $w_1...w_n$. These weights are used to make a prediction, z, using the sigmoid as a classification function. Each round of training works on a few dozen samples and measures the quality of the predictions that are based on the current feature weights. The cross-entropy loss is a measure of how much error the model produces. We want to minimize the total error.

$$\text{Binary Cross Entropy }(y, \hat{y}) = \sum -y\log(\hat{y}) - (1-y)\log(1-\hat{y}) \qquad (2.11)$$

The equation above is the equivalent of finding $p(y|x)$ for each training sample. Thus, we are summing across the labels, y, to have a measure across many samples. In the notation here, y is the correct class and $\hat{y}$ is the predicted class. Because there are only two classes, the probability of one class is represented as $\log(y)$; and the other class is $\log(1-y)$. In other words, every sample that does not belong to Class A must belong to Class B.

We could imagine the classifier getting a first batch of reviews which all share a feature like *awful*, perhaps because they were written by the same author. If a single feature is present in all negative samples for a training batch, the classifier will learn a high weight for that feature. But high feature weights are less likely to generalize; for example, they would fail to describe reviews which do not include *awful*.

$$L_2 \text{ Regularization} = \sum_{w_1...w_i} w^2 \qquad (2.12)$$

For this reason, logistic regression also often uses a regularization method, such as L_2 **Regularization**. This value is the sum of the square of all feature weights. In other words, if one feature has a high weight (like 10) and the other features have a low weight (like 1), this regularization will reduce that overused feature. So, this is a method for helping the classifier to avoid relying on just a few features. The regularization term is added to the optimization function above (binary cross-entropy loss), so that high feature weights are associated with worse models. For example, features weights $1.1, 1.4, 0.75$ have an L_2 term of $1.21 + 3.17 + 0.56 = 4.94$. But alternate feature weights $0.98, 0.75, 0.12$ have an L_2 term of $0.96 + 0.56 + 0.01 = 1.53$. This is how a regularization term can keep the classifier from relying too much on just a few features, by encouraging lower weights as part of the objective function.

A final parameter that you might encounter with logistic regression is the method of dealing with multiple classes. For example, our hotel review problem has just two classes (HIGH and LOW), so the sigmoid classification function works well. But we have other problems, like authorship analysis, that have a fairly large number of classes. In these cases, one option that many implementations use is called **One-vs-Rest** or OVR, in which the classifier is actually made up of a separate classifier for each class. A different option, which we will see in the next section, is to use a different classification function than the sigmoid.

Even with these parameters to set, classifiers like logistic regression are generally well understood and the default settings used in the code notebooks above and the *text_analytics* package will generally work well for problems in corpus linguistics.

It is worth reviewing the details for logistic regression in this section before continuing. We will see these same mechanisms in future models: feature weights, a classification function, an optimization function, and a regularization term. In Section 2.7, feed-forward networks can be seen as expansions on some of these core ideas. And, in Section 3.5, word embeddings use the feature weights from a logistic regression classifier to represent the distribution of words as part of distributional semantics.

2.7 Feed-Forward Networks

A feed-forward network is the most basic kind of deep neural network. These models are also sometimes called a *multi-layer preceptron* or an MLP. It turns out that deep neural networks like this can be seen as an extension of logistic regression. You will remember that a logistic regression classifier makes predictions by multiplying each feature value (our vector representation of language) by a feature weight, represented in the equation below with dot product notation. Together with a bias term, this produces a single float or scalar value for each sample: Values above the decision line belong to one class and values below it belong to another class. The predicted class here, $\hat{y}$, is the output of the classifier. And the classifier itself is a function, $f(x)$, which maps between input representations (x) and output labels ($\hat{y}$).

$$\hat{y} = f(x) = x \cdot w + b \qquad\qquad (2.13)$$

A deep neural network can be viewed as an expansion of this equation, given below. In this notation, $\hat{y}$ is the predicted class, the output of the classifier. And $f(x)$ is the function or model that is applied to our input vector in order to make this prediction. So a feed-forward network expands on logistic regression by adding this $\phi(x)$ term. This part of the model creates a **trainable** intermediate representation between the input (our vector) and the output (our summed feature weights). This intermediate representation is trainable in the sense that it is updated as part of the training process (Goldberg, 2017).

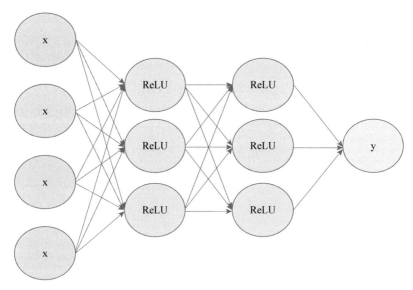

Figure 6 Visualization of a feed-forward network

$$\hat{y} = f(x) = \phi(x) \cdot w + b \tag{2.14}$$

This is visualized in Figure 6, which shows that the model starts with the input vector (*x*) and ends with the prediction layer (*y*), where the prediction layer is similar to the summed feature weights used in logistic regression. The main difference with a deep neural network is that there are multiple **hidden layers** between the input and the output. Each of these hidden layers contains a variable number of *neurons*, each with a particular type of activation.

One common type of activation for neurons in these hidden layers is the sigmoid – exactly the same classification function that we used for logistic regression. Another common activation, the one which we use in the code notebooks, is called the **ReLU activation**. As shown below, this is a very simple neuron which works by replacing negative values with 0.

$$ReLU(x) = max(0,x) \tag{2.15}$$

A feed-forward network is fully connected, meaning that each input value (*x*) is connected with each neuron in the hidden layer. Thus, if we have 500 dimensions in our input vector and 100 neurons in a hidden layer, then the model has 500 ∗ 100 = 50,000 parameters. Logistic regression, on the other hand, has only 500 parameters for the same input (one weight for each feature). In Figure 6, we have just four input features (*x*), two hidden layers with three neurons each (*ReLU*), and a single output node (*y*).

Why would we want a model to have so many trainable parameters? The ideal hypothetical situation is that these intermediate representations that are trained as part of the hidden layers are themselves a form of linguistic analysis. For example, let's think about sentiment in hotel reviews again. It might be the case that some so-called positive words like *amazing* are often used sarcastically: In some contexts they are positive but in other contexts they are negative.

The ideal situation is that the feed-forward network learns some notion of sarcasm or metaphor in its intermediate representation. This is the ideal situation because the actual fact is that we do not know what these intermediate representations contain (which is why they are called hidden layers). A recent trend in natural language processing is to **probe** these layers in order to find out exactly what information from the linguistic signal the network is picking up (Mueller et al., 2020). But such methods are beyond the scope of this section.

So far we have seen that a feed-forward network is like an extension of logistic regression, with a trainable function that maps between the input (x) and the output (y) using hidden layers that contain neurons. These neurons are similar to classification functions and the two sets of terms often overlap. But how does a feed-forward network deal with problems, like authorship analysis, that have more than one class? If we have a binary classification problem with a feed-forward network, we use the sigmoid as the final prediction layer (just like logistic regression). But if we have a multi-class problem, we use the **softmax** as the final prediction layer.

$$softmax\,(z_i) = \frac{e^{z_i}}{\sum_{j=1}^{K} e^{z_j}} \tag{2.16}$$

The softmax is a generalization of the sigmoid classification function. Instead of a single scalar value, it produces a vector of values: one for each class in our problem. You will remember that z is the output layer. Since the softmax is for multiple classes, z is a vector. For example, z_i could be the class DICKENS in our authorship example. The softmax is thus the exponent of that value to the base e, divided by the sum of all values of e^{z_j} for each class in our model. In practical terms, the softmax normalizes the output layer to produce a vector of class probabilities. If the classifier thinks that the best class is DICKENS, the probability in the class vector for DICKENS will contain the highest value. To summarize, then, the *sigmoid* makes binary predictions with a single float and the *softmax* makes multi-class predictions with a vector of floats, each representing the probability of a single class.

The binary cross-entropy loss that we used for logistic regression was focused on just two classes. When we use the softmax in a multi-class problem, we also change the optimization function that we use to measure how much error the classifier is making during training. Here we will use the **categorical cross-entropy loss**. Remember that the output is a vector of probabilities for each possible class ($\hat{y}$). Only one position in that vector is the correct class, represented here as $\hat{y}_{[t]}$. So the categorical cross-entropy loss is the negative log of the predicted probability for what should be the correct class. If that class is not predicted, the probability will be low and thus its negative log will be large (thus, meaning that the model has more error). As before, the classifier wants to minimize this optimization function. The best model is the one which makes the least amount of error.

$$\textit{Categorical Cross Entropy } (\hat{y}, y) = -\log(\hat{y}_{[t]}) \qquad (2.17)$$

In what situations would we use logistic regression (a **shallow** classifier) or a feed-forward network (a **deep** classifier)? First, logistic regression is simpler and it is often best to start with the simplest method. For some problems, we care about *why* the classifier is making its predictions. For example, in authorship problems we might want to know what features a specific author uses or we might want to use the unmasking method to find out how robust the classifier is (see Section 4.3). In these cases, logistic regression allows us to inspect the feature weights and find out which features are being used. But it is not possible to inspect the hidden layers of a feed-forward network.

If we have a small amount of data, it is unlikely that a feed-forward network will be able to learn a good model. But, if we have a very large corpus for training, it is unlikely that logistic regression will continue to improve after a certain point. After all, logistic regression can only learn a single weight for each feature, while a feed-forward network can learn potentially complex representations as part of its hidden layers. So, we might prefer a feed-forward network if we have a large corpus to work with.

The notebook for this section revisits some of our previous classification problems, this time using a feed-forward network. We will see logistic regression in future sections because we use this same architecture to train word embeddings. And we will see feed-forward networks again because we can combine them with word embeddings to create models with multiple layers.[15]

2.8 Ethics: Implicit Bias

This final section on text classification considers the ethical problem of implicit bias. We have so far evaluated text classifiers on held-out data using standard metrics like precision, recall, and f-score. These metrics are important

---

[15] Lab 2.7 –> https://doi.org/10.24433/CO.3402613.v1

for understanding how well the classifier performs. And we have used optimization functions like binary cross-entropy and categorical cross-entropy to measure the error produced by the classifiers during training. But the problem of implicit bias would not necessarily be identified using these measures: We have to remember that a classifier can learn more than we want it to learn.

This is especially true when we have increasingly powerful models (like feed-forward networks) that are trained on increasingly large corpora (containing billions of words). No linguist could read through these corpora, and we know that text data contains many irrelevant cues or heuristic patterns. If a model under-fits the data, the standard metrics like the f-score will be low. But if a model over-fits the data, those metrics might not let us know.

We do not always know why a classifier works. For example, logistic regression allows us to at least inspect the feature weights; but a feed-forward network has hidden layers that we cannot inspect. It is possible that such models will appear to perform well when they are actually learning irrelevant cues. For example, we might think that we can predict what an author's favorite food is, only to later realize that people around the world prefer different foods. So we are actually predicting dialect or native language, together with a small inventory of writers. An American dialect means the author likes burgers; a British accent means the author likes fish and chips.

The problem is that if a classifier learns accidental cues from one corpus, it will fail to generalize to new corpora in which those cues are missing. We have different techniques to avoid learning the wrong cues. But the most important idea is to use large corpora for testing and to design valid categorization systems. We will take a closer look at how to validate classifiers in Section 4.2. Here we explore the problem of implicit bias from an ethical perspective.

In many cases we train a classifier on whatever available corpus contains the ground-truth categories that we need. For example, we trained a classifier to predict the rating given by hotel reviews. The data we used is the data that we had available, an arbitrary selection method. But models tend to slowly degrade as we move away from the training data. If we train on reviews from 2012, the model will tend to perform worse in 2018. And by 2022 it might not work at all. If we train on reviews in the USA, the model will tend to perform worse in New Zealand. And in China it might not work at all. This means that although the promise of computational linguistic analysis is to automate corpus analysis, we still need to perform error analysis for the life of a model to make sure it continues to work well.

We often set up a classifier evaluation using a test set that contains balanced classes: as many news articles about corruption as news articles not about corruption, for example. But, in a real-world setting, some classes will be much more frequent. Most articles from a newspaper will have nothing to do with corruption. This means that many categorization problems are skewed, with relatively small numbers of one category. Minority classes can cause problems as the size of the majority categories increases. For example, a language like te reo Māori (MRI) is so seldom used in digital contexts that, for the task of language identification, most samples that are predicted to belong to MRI are actually false positives.

And this is a problem that extends beyond prediction accuracy. Another difficulty with implicit bias for minority classes is that the classifier can learn what a class is *not* without ever learning what that class *is*. For example, te reo Māori is the Indigenous language in New Zealand and we might train a text classifier to distinguish between MRI and ENG for corpora from New Zealand.[16] But given how skewed the training data is, the likely situation is that the text classifier will actually learn a model for ENG and NOT-ENG. If we tried to use that same classifier in Samoa or Indonesia, it would identify a range of different languages as MRI. Because the assumption during training is that MRI = NON-ENG. And that assumption is not valid outside of the New Zealand context.

3 Text Similarity

3.1 Categorization and Cognition

Human cognition is based on prototype examples, not on the discrete categories that a classifier requires. So far our approach to corpus analysis has required categories with discrete boundaries that are defined in advance: like part of a novel that is either by Dickens or not by Dickens, or a word token that is either a noun or a verb. The problem is that many aspects of human cognition are not categorical: There are not always discrete boundaries between categories, not all members of a category are equally good examples of that category, and there is a hierarchy, with some categories considered BASIC (Taylor, 2004). As a result, many linguistic phenomena need to be modeled without the assumption of strict categorization. In this section we will see how to do this using text similarity models, with a focus on comparison problems.

For categorization problems, using text classification, we can make predictions about samples in isolation. For example, we can predict that a word is a noun, that a document is written in American English, or that a hotel review is positive. A categorization problem is about choosing which of our existing labels best applies to a given sample. But for comparison problems, we make predictions about a continuous (scalar) relationship between two samples: How

---

[16] https://github.com/jonathandunn/eng_mri

close is the sentiment of two reviews, how similar is the distribution of two words, or how comparable are two corpora?

Text similarity models, then, generally involve taking two samples as input and returning a single scalar prediction about their relationship. We can then convert these pairwise similarity relationships into clusters and networks of related items. For example, we will see how to cluster words into semantic domains based on their distribution in a corpus. As soon as we construct that cluster, we are back to a discrete category with fixed boundaries. However, we have not defined those clusters in advance and we can still say which samples are at the center of the cluster, the prototypes.

We start this section by looking at corpus similarity measures (Section 3.2). These measures find relationships between entire data sets using the same type of frequency vectors that we used for text classification. We will use corpus similarity to explore register variation across a dozen languages. We then look at similarity relationships within a corpus using document similarity to find related texts (Section 3.3). As before, *similarity* here can be based on different parts of the linguistic signal: content, structure, or sentiment.

We then move to relationships between words, using co-occurrence to find the association between pairs of words (Section 3.4). This is the same method we used previously to find phrases with the PMI. Here, we contrast the PMI with a more precise ΔP measure which takes the direction of association into account. The next step (Section 3.5) is to look at word embeddings created by the *Skip-Gram Negative Sampling* method (SGNS), which is commonly referred to as WORD2VEC. The interesting part about SGNS is that it approximates a word-association matrix using logistic regression. This means that association measures and word embeddings are two different methods of measuring word distribution in a corpus.

Because we are interested in more than simple pairwise relationships between words, we then expand these word similarity methods by using k-means clustering to create discrete groups of related words (Section 3.6). And, finally, we end this section by raising an ethical problem that is created by models of word association (Section 3.7): What happens when word embeddings capture stereotypes in a way that leads to biased associations?

3.2 Measuring Corpus Similarity

Corpus similarity is the broadest conception of a comparison model, telling us the overall similarity between two corpora or sources of text data. Let's take **register** as an example of why corpus similarity is important. Register refers to the linguistic properties of a corpus that are influenced by the context of

Table 12 Accuracy of corpus similarity measures for predicting register

Code	Language	Accuracy	Feature Type
ara	Arabic	94.6%	Word Unigrams
ell	Greek	100%	Character 4-grams
eng	English	93.3%	Character 4-grams
fra	French	96.6%	Word Unigrams
hin	Hindi	96.6%	Character 4-grams
hun	Hungarian	97.3%	Character 4-grams
ind	Indonesian	100%	Word Unigrams
jpn	Japanese	83.3%	Spaceless Char Bigrams
por	Portuguese	97.3%	Word Unigrams
rus	Russian	98.0%	Character 4-grams
spa	Spanish	97.3%	Word Unigrams
zho	Chinese	96.6%	Spaceless Char Bigrams

production. For example, context is an important factor which drives the differences between news articles or political speeches or novels (Biber, 2012). These different linguistic properties are not caused by the content or the author of a text, but by the context of production.

For example, let's consider three distinct registers: social media (represented by tweets), nonfiction articles (represented by Wikipedia), and the web (a heterogenous register). Each of these sources of data, from unique contexts, will be characterized by specific lexical choices or grammatical patterns. We could use a text classifier to distinguish between registers. However, we are more interested in understanding relationships between different contexts of usage. So, instead of a discrete classifier, we will put together a scalar measure for how similar two corpora are (Kilgarriff, 2001).

We could validate this kind of measure by using a threshold to predict which register a given sample belongs to. For example, in Table 12 we show the accuracy for classifying these three registers across twelve languages. In this case, we are using a corpus similarity measure together with a threshold for predicting whether two samples are from the same or different registers.

Overall, this table shows that we have made very good predictions. And these good predictions indicate that the corpus similarity measure is capturing the difference between registers. The prediction accuracy is not our main focus, but it does provide a validation for our continuous similarity measure. As before, this example is reproduced in the code notebook for this section. You can further explore the measures across a number of other languages.

How do we find the similarity between two corpora? The basic idea is to convert the corpora into a shared vector space and then measure the similarity between the resulting vectors. The vector space is again based on word frequency. But now the feature set is chosen by taking the most frequent vocabulary items in each language. We use 5,000 features, creating a vector of 5,000 dimensions or columns to represent each corpus. The final step is to calculate similarity using Spearman's *rho*, a measure of the correlation between two vectors.

This family of similarity measures has been shown to be quite robust across languages (Dunn, 2021). As we see in Table 12, languages do differ in the specific features that best represent them: Some languages work well with word frequencies and others with character n-gram frequencies. A **character n-gram** is a sequence of characters within a word. So, for example, *goin* and *oing* are both character 4-grams derived from the word *going*. The specific configurations for each language are reproduced from an existing Python package.[17] This means that there is a stable vector space for each language that contains the same vocabulary of features regardless of the corpora being compared.

$$r_s = 1 - \frac{6 \sum d_i^2}{n(n^2 - 1)} \tag{3.1}$$

In the equation for the Spearman correlation, r_s, we have first converted the frequency vector into rank order: the most frequent word in a corpus is 1 and the second most frequent word is 2 and so on. The variable n is the total number of features, here 5,000. And, for each word in the vocabulary, d_i^2 is the squared difference between that word's rank in each corpus. For example, if the feature *were* is the 12th most frequent in one sample and the 20th most frequent in another, the result is $(12 - 20)^2 = 64$. The more similar the word ranks are, the closer to 1 the overall value becomes.

For a text classifier, we convert each sample into a shared vector space and provide those vectors, together with their gold-standard labels, to the classifier. But here we compute the similarity directly from the frequency ranks themselves. On the one hand, logistic regression learns a weight for each feature in the vector space, giving some features more importance overall. Here, we give each feature the same influence. On the other hand, both methods convert a vector of feature values (frequencies) into a single scalar value (here, similarity).

Because this measure is continuous, we do not require fixed boundaries between registers. This is helpful because we might see, for example, movie

---

[17] https://github.com/jonathandunn/corpus_similarity

subtitles that mimic the language of news articles, or news articles that mimic conversational speech. Thus, a continuous measure is more helpful for understanding networks of relationships within and between corpora. Because this measure does not require training data, we are not confined to the registers that we started with. This is helpful because we can continue to use a corpus similarity measure on new kinds of data in a way that would not be appropriate with a text classifier.

You will notice that, previously, we focused our vector representations on a specific part of the linguistic signal. For syntactic patterns, we used function word n-grams or the frequency of constructions. For lexical patterns, we removed stopwords, joined phrases using PMI, and highlighted distinctive terms using TF-IDF. But here we have joined lexical and syntactic features into a single vector by relying on the 5,000 most frequent words. This works very well for corpus similarity, and for register variation in particular, because the context of production influences both lexical and syntactic choices. Finally, the Spearman correlation focuses on difference in frequency ranks, rather than the presence or absence of specific features.

Although this corpus similarity measure is quite accurate across languages, its central tendency varies significantly. For example, samples in Swedish have an average similarity that is much higher than samples in Estonian. When we compare registers across languages, as in Figure 7, we convert each language into a standardized space using the **z-score**. The equation for this, shown below,

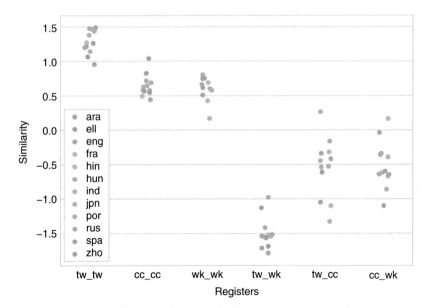

Figure 7 Visualization of corpus similarity by register and language

is simply the population mean (all similarity scores for this language) subtracted from a given sample's score and divided by the standard deviation for the population (again, all similarity scores for this language). This converts each language's similarity values into a standard range. This, in turn, allows us to visualize patterns across many languages. The mean is now 0; values above the mean are more similar than average and values below the mean are less similar than average.

$$z = \frac{(x - \mu)}{\sigma} \tag{3.2}$$

Figure 7 shows the standardized similarity values for many samples across twelve languages. There are three sets of same-register pairs (TW_TW, CC_CC, WK_WK) and three sets of cross-register pairs (TW_WK, TW_CC, CC_WK). Here, TW refers to social media data, CC refers to web data, and WK refers to Wikipedia data. Each dot is one language, averaged across many pairs of subcorpora. Values toward the top (1.5 in standardized space) are very similar, while values toward the bottom (-1.5 in standardized space) are very different. Languages are represented by the color of the dots. For example, Arabic is pinkish.

First, we see that same-register pairs are clearly distinguished from cross-register pairs; this is why we can predict whether two samples come from the same register with such high accuracy. Second, we see that relationships between registers vary. For example, tweets constitute the most self-similar register. And tweets and Wikipedia articles are the most dissimilar, with the lowest values. This means that these two registers are the furthest apart, a relationship that holds across all languages. Finally, web data seems to be the most heterogeneous, with the broadest dispersion of similarity values.

In addition to relationships between registers, we can also use corpus similarity measures to represent the **homogeneity** of a data set. How stable or consistent is a particular corpus? The idea here is to break a much larger corpus into smaller chunks and measure the similarity between random pairs of chunks. If a corpus is quite consistent, the similarity values are high and densely centered around the mean. But, if a corpus is heterogeneous, the similarity values are lower and have a higher variance.

This is a useful way to validate our data, becoming important as we come to rely on very large digital corpora. We visualize the homogeneity of tweets for four languages in Figure 8 using box plots. Here we see that Arabic and Greek are much more densely clustered than English and French, showing a narrower range of variation. English is one of the most heterogeneous languages, likely a result of the diverse population of dialects and varieties that contribute to its

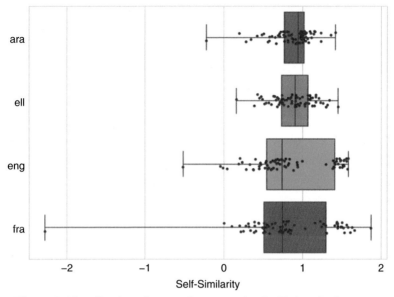

Figure 8 Visualization of corpus homogeneity for Twitter by language

digital usage. In this case, however, the social media data is restricted to a single country in order to control for geographic variation.

This section has looked at a scalar measure for comparing corpora, which we have used to explore different digital registers. This measure creates a frequency-based vector space to represent each subset of a corpus and then compares these vectors using rank correlation. The lab for this section shows how to work with corpus similarity measures across many languages.[18]

3.3 Measuring Document Similarity

Now let's move beyond corpus similarity and look at a smaller unit of analysis: documents. The question here is, which texts are the most similar? Given our approach to representing different parts of the linguistic signal as a vector, *similarity* here can mean three different things: content-based similarity (reviews of the same hotel), author-based similarity (reviews written by the same kind of tourist), or sentiment-based similarity (very favorable reviews of different hotels). The linguistic signal, a text, carries all three pieces of information. And so when we measure document similarity, we start by using exactly the same representations that we have used for text classification. For content, we represent a text using TF-IDF weighting with stopwords removed and PMI to

---

[18] Lab 3.2 –> https://doi.org/10.24433/CO.3402613.v1

find phrases. For authorship, we represent a text using function word n-grams. And, for sentiment, we represent a text using positive and negative sentiment words.

Previously, we used content features to classify tweets from different cities, stylistic features to classify different nineteenth-century writers, and sentiment features to classify hotel reviews. We will use those same features and corpora here. But, instead of training a classifier using predefined discrete labels, we only measure the pairwise similarity between documents. Those documents which are closer in vector space are more similar. Those which are further apart in vector space are less similar. When we create a vector space that highlights syntax or semantics, we focus document similarity on that part of the linguistic signal.

We will use a common metric called Euclidean distance to measure how far apart two vectors are. You will notice that distance and similarity are the same measure from different perspectives, depending on whether 0 means very little overlap or very little difference. So, we calculate the distance between vectors representing our texts in order to measure the distance between the texts themselves. Distance is different from a measure of correlation such as that which we used for corpus similarity, but the overall paradigm of comparing vector representations is the same.

Let's say we have two documents, A and B. We are using sentiment words, so for each document we have a vector of a few thousand frequency values. These vectors are like rows in a table. Each column is a word like *enjoyed* or *endured*. The formula for calculating distance in this context is shown below. We take the difference between each column and square it. So, we calculate how many times *enjoyed* occurs in document A (2) minus how many times *enjoyed* occurs in document B (1). The result is 1; and 1^2 is still 1. Then we add all these columns together and take the square root. When the formula says A_n, it means that we do this same pairwise comparison across every column in our table of vectors.

$$distance\,(A,B) = \sqrt{(A_1 - B_1)^2 + (A_2 - B_2)^2 \cdots + (A_n - B_n)^2} \qquad (3.3)$$

In other words, the method for calculating Euclidean distance is the same for 5 features or 5,000 features. Squaring each comparison eliminates the direction of the distance (positive or negative). Features with a higher value (like distinctive words when we use TF-IDF), have more impact on the overall measure. For example, if *tulip* occurs zero times in one document and thirty-four times in another document, this large gap will have a large influence: $(34-0)^2 = 1,156$. A measure like Euclidean distance allows more frequent items to have more influence on the final similarity value.

Table 13 Author similarity results

Target	#1	#2	#3	#4	#5
Bennett	Bennett	Bennett	Bennett	Bennett	Bennett
Abbott	Abbott	Abbott	Abbott	Abbott	Abbott
Altsheler	Altsheler	Altsheler	Altsheler	Altsheler	Altsheler

Table 14 City similarity results

Target	#1	#2	#3	#4	#5
Calgary	Calgary	Calgary	Calgary	Calgary	Calgary
Brisbane	Melbourne	Adelaide	Perth	Adelaide	Brisbane
Washington	Wash.	Wash.	Wash.	Wash.	Wash.
Mumbai	Mumbai	Mumbai	Bengaluru	Mumbai	Mumbai

Euclidean distance gives us a single measure of similarity for any two documents. And yet there are thousands of dimensions in the case of sentiment analysis. So our high-dimensional vector is being compressed into a single distance measure. This might be reductive if we only had two texts. But we have a whole network of relationships, because we can measure the linguistic distance between every pair of texts. The more samples (documents) that we have, the more we know about each one: We also know about the relationships that document has with every other document.

Let's start with authorship and style. We have seen that we can classify nineteenth-century writers quite well, making highly accurate predictions using function word n-grams. What happens if we try to search for similar writers using Euclidean distance to compare texts?

We randomly choose one sample, one chapter of a book. We end up with five other chapters written by the same author. This works, in Table 13, for Bennett, Abbott, and Altsheler. As always, you can explore this further in the code notebooks. This consistency will likely not always be observed for each sample, but the overall trend is clear.

Next we look at cities. We used a text classifier to predict which city tweets are from. If we use similarity measures based on the same content features, what would we find? Here in Table 14 we have four examples: In two cases (Calgary and Washington, DC), each of the five most similar samples come from the same city. In the other two cases, we have imperfect predictions that reveal larger patterns. For example, the most common samples for Brisbane

Table 15 Sentiment similarity results

Target	#1	#2	#3	#4	#5
HIGH	HIGH	HIGH	HIGH	HIGH	HIGH
LOW	LOW	LOW	LOW	LOW	HIGH

(in Australia) are other cities from Australia. And the most common samples for Mumbai are Mumbai and another Indian city, Bengaluru. This shows why similarity measures are important: We can ask questions that go beyond discrete boundaries to find out what the relationships are between samples.

Does the same pattern occur with sentiment analysis? Here we use positive and negative words to find the most similar hotels based on reviews. We display the target with its most similar hotels using their labels: HIGH or LOW. We see, in Table 15, that the documents which are most similar from a linguistic perspective are also the most similar given their properties in the external world.

To summarize, we have converted documents into vector space, focusing on content, style, or sentimeant. And then we have used Euclidean distance to search for similar documents in that vector space, given an exemplar that we want to start with. This idea of starting with an exemplar is an approximation for how humans structure categories. Our lab for this section shows how to search for the most similar documents given a particular type of representation.[19]

3.4 Measuring Word Similarity Using Association

The methods described above tell us about the similarity between two documents in content, style, or sentiment. How could we measure the similarity between words, a much smaller span of language? In this section we look at **association measures**, a way of measuring the probability that a sequence of words occurs together. The basic idea is that words which are likely to occur together in a corpus have an association, and this association reflects a shared meaning or an idiomatic meaning.

We previously used Pointwise Mutual Information, or PMI, to find phrases. But PMI does not take directional information into account. For example, consider the phrase *of course* in (12). The probability of *course* given *of* is rather small from left to right, because *of* is quite common and occurs with many other words. But the probability of *course* given *of* is quite high from right to

---
[19] Lab 3.3 –> https://doi.org/10.24433/CO.3402613.v1

Table 16 Variables for calculating the ΔP

	Y Present (Y_P)	Y Absent (Y_A)	TOTALS
X Present (X_P)	a	b	a + b
X Absent (X_A)	c	d	c + d
TOTALS	a + c	b + d	

left, because *course* is not preceded by a wide variety of words. This means that the left-to-right association is rather low, but the right-to-left association is rather high. The PMI does not capture this distinction.

(12) The game will *of course* be finished by that time.

Here we introduce a measure of association that captures the probability that two words co-occur from both directions, called the ΔP (Dunn, 2018c; Ellis, 2007; Gries, 2013). This probability is based on the frequency of words observed in a corpus, as shown in Table 16. Taking *of course* as our example, the variable *a* represents the frequency of those two words together. The variable *b* represents just *of* on its own and *c* represents just *course* on its own. To control for the size of the corpus, a final variable *d* captures the number of words in the corpus that do not include *of course*. A further advantage over the PMI is that negative or very low values also have an interpretation: Two words are likely not to occur together, to repel each other.

Given these frequency-based variables, the two variants of the ΔP are shown below. In the first case, we take the probability that *course* follows *of* adjusted by the probability that some other word follows *of*. And, in the second case, we take the probability that *of* comes before *course*, adjusted by the probability that *course* is preceded by some other word. Taken together, these two measures provide a more nuanced view of the association between *of* and *course*, including the variety of other options that are available.

$$\Delta P_{LR} = \frac{a}{a+c} - \frac{b}{b+d} \qquad (3.4)$$

$$\Delta P_{RL} = \frac{a}{a+b} - \frac{c}{c+d} \qquad (3.5)$$

We start by using the ΔP to find the most associated phrases in a corpus. Table 17 shows association from the corpus of tweets and web pages (on the top), contrasted with the corpus of nineteenth-century books (on the bottom). In addition to the left-to-right and right-to-left variants, we show a *Frequency* value, which represents the number of occurrences. A table like this is a simple way to find collocations in a data set. Here we are looking at words with a

Table 17 ΔP Association, phrases with high left-to-right attraction

Corpus	Phrase	LR	RL	Freq
Tweets+Web	luther vandross	0.93	0.05	218
Tweets+Web	white flippered	0.92	0.00	12
Tweets+Web	a nutshell	0.90	0.00	2,074
Tweets+Web	lucille lortel	0.99	0.04	22
PG Books	king bucar	0.99	0.00	20
PG Books	de mauves	0.92	0.00	226
PG Books	the huberts	0.91	0.00	92
PG Books	a goner	0.96	0.00	132

Table 18 ΔP association, phrases with high right-to-left attraction

Corpus	Phrase	LR	RL	Freq
Tweets+Web	blackstorm labs	0.00	0.92	13
Tweets+Web	doled out	0.00	0.95	173
Tweets+Web	kumsusan palace	0.00	0.99	44
Tweets+Web	specialise in	0.00	0.90	2,576
PG Books	interdigital pits	0.00	0.99	18
PG Books	regardless of	0.00	0.90	6,946
PG Books	addiction to	0.00	0.90	276
PG Books	walmington square	0.00	0.99	16

high left-to-right but low right-to-left association. This includes names (*luther vandross*) but also phrases (*a nutshell, a goner*).

While the PMI makes no distinction between directions of association, Table 18 now shows phrases with the opposite configuration: a high right-to-left association. Here we see different types of names (*blackstorm labs, walmington square*) and different types of phrases (*doled out, regardless of*). This shows the greater nuance that we get by using the ΔP.

Our first approach to **vector semantics** is to use this matrix of association values to represent each word. Theses tables are sparse matrices because we are only including pairs with a high value; a complete matrix would show the association between every pair of words. This, in fact, is the starting point for popular approaches to vector semantics like latent semantic analysis (Landauer, Foltz, & Laham, 1998) or global vectors (Pennington, Socher, & Manning, 2014). If we are interested in phrases and collocations, association measures applied to multi-word sequences, as we have done here, are a useful tool. But, if we are interested in finding relationships between words, a network of association values is the next step.

When we calculate an association matrix, we look at frequencies for the entire corpus for each possible pair of words. This means that the resulting matrix is stable: We always get the same output when we observe the same corpus. But it also means that we have to keep a very large number of very infrequent pairs in memory, making this approach consistent but resource intensive. In the lab for this section, we work with the ΔP measure in more detail.[20]

3.5 Measuring Word Similarity in Vector Space

We have been representing language (words, documents, corpora) as vectors in order to compare and model those vectors as a proxy for comparing the language itself. When we do this with words, we call it VECTOR SEMANTICS. The basic idea is that the relationships between words that we expect from lexical semantics (synonymy, meronymy, metonymy, etc.) should now be captured in vector space. Because these vectors are based on co-occurrences, we also call this DISTRIBUTIONAL SEMANTICS. But the idea is the same: Words that have the same distributions, that occur in the same contexts, should have the same vector representations. This means that, again, the vector representation is a proxy that indicates which words have similar meanings.

In practice, vector semantics is more limited than lexical semantics. These methods tend to be quite good at finding which words are related to one another. But comparing vectors, for example using Euclidean distance, does not allow us to distinguish between different types of relationship like synonymy and meronymy. You will notice as we work through lists of related words that these lists represent many distinct types of semantic relationships.

The challenge here is to measure the distribution of words. Instead of looking at the entire corpus at once to calculate an association matrix, the word2vec algorithm trains a logistic regression classifier using stochastic gradient descent. This is the same architecture that we used previously for text classification; but instead of using logistic regression to make discrete predictions, we are using its weights as part of vector semantics. More precisely, we are discussing the *Skip-Gram Negative Sampling* variant of word2vec (Mikolov et al., 2013). There is a close theoretical relationship between this approach to vector semantics and approaches based on a matrix of association values (Levy, Goldberg, & Dagan, 2015).

---

[20] Lab 3.4 –> https://doi.org/10.24433/CO.3402613.v1

Let's say we have a very large data set, like all lead paragraphs from *The New York Times* over a period of eighty-five years. This provides millions and millions of sentences, enough to estimate the distribution of even relatively infrequent words. The word2vec algorithm is based on predicting co-occurrence: What words occur within five words to the left and right of CAT? For example, in (13a) through (13c) the target word is shown in bold and the words within the context window are shown in italics. The basic idea is to train a model to predict which words fall within that context. So, the goal is to predict that *stray* and *person* and *training* are words that go along with the target word CAT. You will notice that many of the words in the context window are actually stopwords (function words). Most implementations of word2vec remove stopwords before finding the words inside the context window. This is a method used to focus on the content of the sentence rather than its structure or style.

(13a) Our neighborhood has an increasing *number of stray* [**cats**].

(13b) My aunt is *a really big* [**cat**] *person; she just* loves them.

(13c) We did a good job *of training the* [**cat**] *to not scratch* the couch.

The goal is to train a logistic regression classifier that predicts which words will occur in the context window (i.e., which words will show up in italics). The positive class is made up of those words which are actually observed in the context for each word. The negative class is made up of randomly chosen words which do not occur in the context window. This is called **negative sampling**. In general, the algorithm works well when trained with a large number of negative samples for each positive sample. The reason is that most words do not co-occur, so there are more negative examples than positive examples in a full corpus.

When we created previous vector representations, each dimension or column represented a particular vocabulary item: a word, an n-gram, a sequence of characters, or a construction. But in word2vec the dimensions do not represent any particular linguistic feature. They are purely properties of the model, logistic regression. The equation for logistic regression is repeated below, where the prediction z is a dot product of the features and the feature weights. In word2vec, each word is represented by a set of feature weights. During training, these weights are optimized to make predictions about the context of the word. After training, these weights are exported as the vector representation for that word.

$$z = w \cdot x + b \tag{3.6}$$

This is a form of **semi-supervised learning**. The model is trained to make predictions about a ground truth, but the ground truth does not require any annotation or labeling. And we are not directly interested in the prediction task itself, at least not to the same degree that we are interested in the final word embeddings that come from the feature weights.

What exactly is the underlying prediction task here? The model needs to ensure that the probability of the positive examples (which actually occur) is higher than the probability of the negative examples (which we sampled randomly from the vocabulary). When the predictions are incorrect, the stochastic gradient descent algorithm changes the feature weights (the future word embeddings) to correct that error. In other words, the prediction task for the classifier is semi-supervised because it is learning to predict a quality that is not what we are actually interested in.

$$Prediction = P(target|context) \qquad (3.7)$$

How do we know the probability that is referred to above, that a target word is observed given a specific context? The skip-gram negative sampling algorithm calculates the similarity between the current vector (the feature weights) for both the target word and the context words (where the context words include both the positive and negative examples). We talked about Euclidean distance in Section 3.3; this algorithm uses an alternate distance measure called **cosine distance**. This is the dot product of each current word embedding: The feature weights are multiplied together, element by element. The cosine is normalized by the multiplied absolute values of the two vectors to reduce the impact of very large values. This is important because otherwise the word embeddings for very common words like *the* or *seems* would be given more weight than the embeddings for rare words.

$$cosine\,(t, c) = \frac{t \cdot c}{|t| * |c|} \qquad (3.8)$$

So the cosine distance between the target word (CAT) and each of the context words (real positive examples and fake negative examples) is used to estimate the probability that they co-occur. The goal is for the positive examples to end up with a high probability and the negative examples to end up with a low probability. As with logistic regression before, the sigmoid function is used to convert this probability (the cosine similarity) into a prediction. Values above 0.5 are positive predictions and values below 0.5 are negative predictions.

Let's compare this with an association-based approach to vector semantics. For a word association matrix, we take the entire corpus into memory and calculate the association (probability) for each possible pair of words based on observed frequency. If we are working with a very large corpus, this becomes a computationally expensive task. The word2vec algorithm approximates this

Table 19 Words similar to *sonnets*

Target	#1	#2	#3	#4	#5
sonnets	verse	poems	Aeschylus	poem	psalms

same association matrix by using logistic regression to make predictions about word contexts. But, importantly, the algorithm only needs to consider one sentence at a time. This means that a single machine can process very large corpora. However, the side effect of this efficiency is that word2vec is less stable. In other words, given a corpus, we will always get the same word association matrix. Nonetheless, we will not always get the same word embeddings (Hellrich, Kampe, & Hahn, 2019). For instance, each pass will have entirely different words used as negative examples for the classifier.

We are going to explore word embeddings by using cosine distance to search for the most similar words. But first we have one more problem to think about. You will notice that vector semantics is based entirely on strings: Every unique string is assumed to be a single word. So, for example, I work at a TABLE. But in a meeting I might TABLE a new motion. Or I'm feeling FINE right now. But only until I get another library FINE. The problem is that word2vec gives us a single embedding even though these strings are actually different words.

Here we use part-of-speech tags, like noun and verb, to distinguish between different word senses. These are the same tags that we trained a text classifier to predict in Section 2.4. So we start by using a part-of-speech tagger to label each word according to its grammatical category. Then we train word embeddings that distinguish between *fine*_N and *fine*_ADJ. That makes our vectors a better representation of word meaning. We show these tags in the code notebooks, but for the sake of space they are removed here.

Now, back to our problem. Let's search to find out which words are the most similar. The target word in Table 19 is abstract, *sonnets*. And the most similar words are other abstract words from the same domain. These words are abstract in the sense that their definition is entirely a matter of social construction (Dunn, 2015). In addition, we have a nonabstract word, a named-entity, *Aeschylus*, who is associated with poetry. This is a good example of the kind of relationships that word2vec captures: words from the same domain, but with a variety of distinct lexical semantic relationships.

Here in Table 20 is another example, words similar to *fisticuffs*. Some of these are adjectives and some verbs; one is a noun (*brawls*). In this case, we have different paraphrases or synonyms, words that could be used in the same context with slightly different nuances.

Table 20 Words similar to *fisticuffs*

Target	#1	#2	#3	#4	#5
fisticuffs	hairpulling	taunting	trashtalking	fist-swinging	brawls

Table 21 Word similarity by corpus

unfairness	#1	#2	#3
NYT	irresponsibility	hypocrisy	excessiveness
Congress	inconsistency	absurdity	inequality

isolationist	#1	#2	#3
NYT	antidemocratic	antiwashington	unilateralist
Congress	defeatist	antimilitary	internationalist

Is there a single vector representation for each word regardless of the corpus that we use for training? The answer is no, which is what we expect given variation in registers and dialects and individuals. Here in Table 21 we contrast two words, using embeddings drawn from the *The New York Times* and embeddings drawn from congressional speeches (both corpora cover the same period of time, 1931 to 2016). The first target is *unfairness*. The news articles find related words like *hypocrisy*, but the congressional corpus finds more abstract words like *inequality*, a slightly different focus. For the second target, *isolationist*, we see a different range of words, each with a different semantic relationship. Some are words with the opposite meaning (*internationalist*) and some are words with a political spin (*anti-democratic, defeatist*).

The point of this section has been that we can use vector semantics, whether from a word association matrix or from an algorithm like word2vec, to represent the distribution of words. The distribution is taken as a proxy for linguistic properties of the word. And then we measure the distance between words in this vector space, allowing us to search for the most similar words in the same way that we previously searched for the most similar documents. These methods are useful for providing domains of related words, even though these domains in fact represent a large number of distinct lexical semantic relationships. In the lab for this section we practice working with word embeddings in more detail.[21]

---

[21] Lab 3.5 –> https://doi.org/10.24433/CO.3402613.v1

3.6 Clustering by Similarity

We have been working to measure the similarity between words and documents and corpora as a way of avoiding the discrete categories that a text classifier requires. But so far we have been looking at pairwise similarities, even when we have access to vector semantics given word embeddings. This means that, in most contexts, we need to consider a very large number of pairs as part of our analysis. Let's expand pairwise similarity across an entire data set by using Euclidean distance to find clusters of related items, focusing on clusters of related words. This means that we can create groups of words that represent a single semantic domain. These clusters are much like the categories produced by a text classifier, except that we as linguists do not define the categories. Instead, we use unsupervised learning to find the clusters.

We will use the k-means clustering algorithm throughout our examples. The algorithm's goal is to find groups of words that minimize within-cluster variance. This means that the words inside a cluster are more similar to each other than they are to words outside the cluster. So we are searching for those groups of words that are most homogeneous.

We define what we mean by homogeneous using Euclidian distance. We start by calculating the **centroid** for each cluster, the exact middle point. This centroid is like the best example of a category. So, a carrot is a really good example of a vegetable and it sits right in the middle of the category VEGETA-BLE. For k-means, the center or prototype for each category is the centroid, the exact middle based on the distances between all the words in that cluster. While there might not be a word in the exact centroid position, we can find the word which is nearest to that centroid position as the prototype or exemplar for the cluster.

But how does the algorithm actually find clusters? First, as shown in Table 22, we initialize the algorithm with our best guess. So we try a couple random clusterings and find out which works best. This clustering becomes the starting point. Then k-means has two basic steps during each iteration. The first step is to reassign each word to the nearest centroid. So if a lemon is closest to the centroid VEGETABLE, then we add it to the VEGETABLE cluster. The second step is to recalculate the centroid based on all the words that are now in that cluster. So, if we add lemon to the VEGETABLE cluster, then that category has been changed, potentially creating a new centroid.

These two simple steps (both based on calculating Euclidean distance) are repeated over and over many times. For each turn, we make a few changes, flipping a word from one cluster to another. We finally stop the algorithm when we stop making any significant changes.

Table 22 Pseudo-code for k-means clustering algorithm

Variables	
define	*tolerance* = The amount that cluster assignments have changed this cycle
define	*word* = A word represented in vector space using word2vec
define	*cluster* = A group of words centered around the mean or centroid
define	*centroid* = The prototype or central example that represents the center point of the cluster

Algorithm	
Loop	WHILE *tolerance* is below our threshold:
Step 1	FOR each word: Assign word to the nearest centroid using squared Euclidean distance
Step 2	FOR each cluster: Recalculate the centroid as the mean of all words that are now in the cluster

The only disadvantage to k-means is that we have to set k in advance: How many clusters do we want? If we want ten clusters, we have to tell the algorithm that $k = 10$. If we want 100 clusters, we have to tell the algorithm that $k = 100$. So, for a text classifier we have to define what the categories are. But for k-means we only have to say how many categories we want to end up with.

Most words have multiple meanings, some of which are completely different. For example, the noun *table* is a place to put things but the verb *to table* is about the formality of including an issue on the agenda for a meeting. Word embeddings, by default, are unable to distinguish between these word senses. As described in the previous section, we can use a part-of-speech tagger that we have already trained to help distinguish between syntactic categories; but this still does not account for polysemy.

To a linguist, different forms of a word like *running* vs *ran* vs *run* are still the same word. Each form marks different properties like tense and aspect. But, from a computational perspective, each of these word forms has a different embedding (because they are each different strings). So while *table* and *table* might be conflated into a single row, *ran* and *run* are divided into separate rows.

Our first example cluster, from embeddings trained from the corpus derived from *The New York Times*, is shown above in Table 23. This is a good example of how word embeddings together with k-means can produce semantic

Table 23 Semantic domain 1, from news articles

living	dining	kitchen	garage
pool	whirlpool	bath	terrace
deck	fireplace	ceilings	floors
renovated	remodeled	patio	porch
maids	doormen	maintenance	concierge

Table 24 Semantic domain 2, from news articles

medical	medicine	clinical	physicians
psychiatry	pediatric	dental	dentistry
psychiatric	pediatrics	orthopedic	pathology
gynecology	obstetrics	cardiology	oncology
surgery	neurology	internship	radiology
ophthalmology	dermatology	immunology	urology
anesthesiology	gastroenterology	hematology	gynecological

domains, here the domain of HOUSE. We see different types of rooms, *living* vs *dining*, and different features, like *pool* and *terrace*. But some of these words are about the condition of the house: *renovated* and *remodeled*. And others are about the staff of a house: *maid* and *doormen*. From a linguistic perspective, these words are related to one another but account for a range of unique semantic relationships.

In our second example, in Table 24, we see different aspects of a MEDICAL PRACTITIONER domain. Some of the terms capture different fields of medicine: *neurology* vs *cardiology*. We also see different forms of the same concept, like *psychiatry* and *psychiatric*. Again, these examples show us that we are working with a broad semantic domain, not with specific lexical relationships. The lab for this section explores in more detail the problem of how to cluster words.[22]

3.7 Ethics: Model Discrimination

What happens if our models learn to discriminate by picking up negative stereotypes? Think about this: Vector semantics assumes that the distribution of words in a large corpus tells us what those words mean. So, *dog* occurs in contexts that include words like *feed* and *pet* and *train* and *walk*. But what if some genders (like *he/his/him*) are more likely to occur in texts about

---

[22] Lab 3.6 –> https://doi.org/10.24433/CO.3402613.v1

computer science than other genders (like *she/hers/her*)? What if some religions (like *Islam/Muslim*) are more likely to occur in texts about terrorism than other religions (like *Judaism/Jewish*)? What if some groups (like *African-American*) are more likely to occur in texts about crime than other groups (like *Asian-American*)? We can pose three questions here.

First, does the meaning of a word actually come from the distribution or usage of that word? If most texts about computer science do not include female pronouns, does that imply masculinity is actually a part of the meaning of computer science? This is an issue of discrimination that is not relevant when we deal with words like *shoe* or *library*. So one ethical question is, which words require an adjustment to make sure that our models do not learn discriminating negative stereotypes?

Second, is the goal of corpus linguistics to learn from actual human behavior or to learn from idealized human behavior? In other words, let's say we learn about the world from billions of tweets. And let's say that discourse on Twitter is sexist and xenophobic and racist. Would a model of vector semantics be wrong to reproduce the actual human ideas that it encounters in a corpus? In other words, is the underlying problem model discrimination or is this simply a reflection of human discrimination?

Third, does every word have a single, most basic meaning? The issue here is that linguistic meaning involves both the speaker and the audience: How do individuals interpret this or that word? Many cases, like *shoe* or *library*, may not have any significant individual variation. A dog is a dog is a dog. Thus, a single vector representation that covers many different populations of speakers may suffice. However, a word embedding, for example, is based on the assumption that there is a single meaning for each word. And we can discover that one true meaning if we analyze enough texts. But if there is variation across populations, then more data will lead to more noise. For example, there are ideas that people fight about, like *freedom* and *justice*. We would end up with very different distributions for these words if we compared, for example, *Fox News* and *The New York Times*. The population of speakers that we use for training influences our final representation of word meaning.

Let's make this discussion less abstract by comparing some word classes that we get using word2vec with k-means clustering, as before using data from *The New York Times*. Here in Table 25 is our first example of a word class. These are all nouns from the semantic domain of TRAVEL. Some words are neutral, like *trip* and *travel*. Other words depend on the purpose of the travel, like *commute* vs *honeymoon*. And still other words depend on our intentions in respect to the destination, like *stranded* vs *sojourn*. So there is, again, a lot of variation in the specific nuances that are encoded within this semantic domain.

Table 25 Semantic domain 3, from news articles

trip	travel	journey	tour
visit	commute	honeymoon	pilgrimage
returning	arriving	depart	stranded
vacation	excursion	detour	sojourn
fly	ride	trek	traveling

Table 26 Semantic domain 4, from news articles

hear	listen	laugh	cry
smile	whisper	clap	wave
kiss	chat	stare	shout
reminisce	tease	cheer	vent
weep	spit	yell	scream
wince	groan	sneer	boo

Table 27 Semantic domain 5, from news articles

victims	prisoners	refugees	immigrants
civilians	terrorists	hostages	foreigners
aliens	asylum	dissidents	hijackers
detainees	Iraqis	Cubans	Iranians

Here in Table 26 is another cluster that shows how these domains can contain a variety of human emotions. Here we have words that involve a social expression of emotion in some way, like *laugh* and *smile*. Some of these are positive (*smile*), some neutral (*chat*), and some negative (*weep*). So this domain is encoding many different emotions together.

The danger is that we start to encode properties that are actually stereotypes of some kind. Here in Table 27 is a cluster that involves a domain of TERRORISM, including words like *victims* and *hostages* and *hijackers*. But it also include named entities like *Iraqis* and *Cubans*.

In other words, these domains are formed by association. And part of the observed distribution of these words involves a negative stereotype. It is important to remember that, although we talk about word embeddings as vector semantics, the underlying method is closely related to measures of association.

Table 28 Semantic domain 6, from news articles

blacks	negroes	african_american
hispanic	latino	spanish_speaking
mexican_american	asian_american	chinese_american
cuban_american	italian_american	arab_american
poorer	poorest	lower_income
immigrant	migrant	foreign_born
sweatshops	farm_workers	undocumented
ghettos	illiterate	impoverished
uneducated	exoffenders	unemployed

And keep in mind that these embeddings come from *The New York Times*. If we were working with social media data, we might be able to blame misinformation or hate speech for these sorts of patterns. But the actual problem is that distributional methods, without any adjustments, tend to **amplify** negative stereotypes, even if the original intent of the texts is to argue against those stereotypes (Zhao et al., 2018).

Table 28 shows another domain from the same corpus. It includes groups which are racial or ethnic minorities in the USA (*blacks, hispanics*). Keep in mind that the corpus ranges from 1931 to 2016, so some terms are used which have become less acceptable over time. Also included in this domain are *migrants*, but not just any migrants: Specifically, it includes migrants with a negative stereotype of some sort. And, at the bottom, also included in this domain, are negative attributes: *poorest, illiterate, uneducated*, and *ex-offenders*.

To be fair, this is not an exhaustive list of terms for this domain; it also includes *whites*, for example. But it is clear that this domain comes from comparing minority groups with a majority categaory. And, whether or not the original texts intend to support negative stereotypes, that is precisely what the word embeddings pick up. Regardless of the overall argument that a particular document makes, the repeated association of words occurring within a particular topic leads to the acquisition of these negative stereotypes.

The main idea in this section has been that computational models can acquire negative stereotypes, partly from the texts used for training and partly from the distributional methods that are used. In and of itself, a model like this could be used to study the association of words. But the ethical problem comes when we base more complicated models on the assumption that vector semantics represents the meaning of words. The basic fact is that distributional semantics represents a corpus, rather than either human cognition or some sort of external reality. The more influence we give such models (for example, using them for search engines or machine translation) and the less transparent the models become, the more we have incorporated discrimination into our linguistic analysis.

4 Validation and Visualization

We have now seen how computational methods can be used to answer both categorization problems and comparison problems. If we want to use these methods to answer linguistic questions, however, we need to give further attention to how we can validate the answers that we get: How can we have confidence in our results when we as linguists cannot individually verify all the corpus data we rely on? Here we discuss how to report results using baselines to provide context (Section 4.1) and how to ensure that our results are robust (Section 4.2). We then turn our focus to visualization methods to further explore our results, working with relational plots (Section 4.3), box plots and heat maps (Section 4.4), and choropleth maps (Section 4.5). As before, we end this section by considering the ethical implications for these computational methods: Here we consider the influence that data availability has on the languages and populations which we are able to study using computational methods.

4.1 Reporting Results for Political Speech Prediction

It is difficult to evaluate how well a computational model is performing in isolation. For example, imagine that we can predict New Zealand English vs Australian English when most samples are from the Australian dialect. This is an imbalanced binary classification problem: *imbalanced* because the majority class (Australian English) dominates and *binary* because there are just two classes. Our baseline expectation for this dialect model would be higher than for a model with twelve dialects (cf. Section 2.1) with an equal number of test samples from each one. In other words, an f-score of 0.50 would be bad in the first case but rather good in the second case. This means that when we evaluate the performance of a model we need some method to contextualize the raw accuracy measures.

In this section, we will be looking at the example of training a text classifier to predict whether a congressional speech was given by a Republican or a Democrat. When do we know that the classifier's performance on this binary classification problem is meaningful? To find out, we first establish a baseline that we can use for comparison, to contextualize the results.

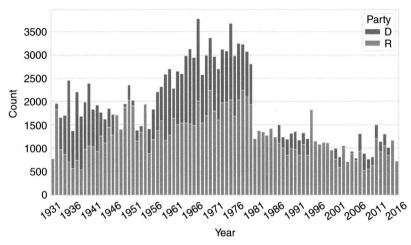

Figure 9 Number of speeches by party, 1931 to 2016, House and Senate

The simplest baseline is to measure the accuracy of guessing the majority class in every case. For example, Figure 9 shows us that, in the 1960s and 1970s, most speeches in congress were by Democrats. The red and blue bars are overlaid, so that in this period there are about 2,000 speeches by Republicans and about 3,000 by Democrats. So, we expect the classifier to work better for Democratic speeches in that period. If 70% of speeches are from Democrats, then our majority baseline for accuracy is 70%: the score we would have gotten by predicting DEMOCRAT for each speech.

We have a very large number of options available for any given kind of corpus analysis: Which representations do we use? Which models? Which data set? Let's say that we are wondering whether it is helpful to remove emojis from tweets. Do they provide useful information or do they create noise? In this case, we would evaluate the performance of these two different settings in an A vs B evaluation: With all other choices the same, is MODEL A or MODEL B better? This method allows us to systematically improve our models.

When we compare multiple models like this, however, we need to use a statistical test to determine whether the difference between MODEL A and MODEL B is actually significant. Figure 10 shows our classification accuracy (the f-score) for the period in question, 1931 to 2016. On the bottom, in blue, is the majority baseline. This is what we would get by predicting the most common class. On the top, in red, is the classifier's f-score. This is what we actually got. So the improvement over the baseline is the difference between the red and blue lines.

In this case, the difference between the two lines is quite clear. But we are not always sure if there actually is a difference. The t-test is a way to measure how significant the difference between two models actually is in a situation, like

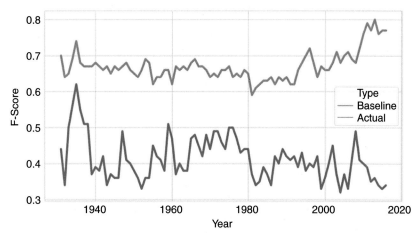

Figure 10 Party classification by year with majority baseline, 1931 to 2016, House only

this, where we have many scores for each condition (actual classifier vs baseline). Here the p-value is less than 0.001. That means there is a very significant difference that we can have confidence in.

For classifying by political party, we take the party labels as our categories. And then we train a classifier to tell us which speeches are written by Republicans and which are written by Democrats. If we just do one classification, for the entire twentieth century, that would not necessarily tell us anything about nonlinguistic attributes of the speeches, like political polarization. But here we train and test a model for each year: How distinct were the parties in 1933 and how distinct were they in 1955?

When polarization is low, it should be more difficult to tell the parties apart just from the text of speeches, because not every Democrat will be taking exactly the same position. But, when polarization is high, it should be easier to tell the parties apart using their speeches because every member of congress is sticking closely to the party line. Thus, when we train a model for each year we can use changes in the prediction accuracy as a proxy for political polarization. The higher the prediction accuracy, the easier it is to tell the parties apart, the more polarized the underlying parties are (Diermeier et al., 2011; Dunn et al., 2016).

In Figure 10, we see that the classifier's performance is well above the baseline for every year, which tells us that the classifier is finding meaningful textual cues for party. But there are also wide fluctuations. Let's test for two statistical properties: First, are the actual performance and the majority baseline correlated? Second, is there a significant difference between them? These results

Table 29 Relationship between majority baseline and classification accuracy

Pearson Correlation	Correlation Significance	T-Test P-Value
-0.114	0.293	0.001

in Table 29 show, first, that the classifier's performance is significantly better than the baseline. This is visually clear, but it is good to confirm that analysis. But this also shows us that there is no significant correlation between the majority baseline (based on which party is dominant in any given year) and the classifier's performance. This means that the distribution of speeches by party is not a factor determining when the classifier works well and when it does not work well. Thus, this indicates that there is a meaningful textual cue for political party.

For these classification results, we have relied on content features (PMI for phrases with TF-IDF weighting); we have refit these features and weightings for each congress. In other words, the vocabulary for 1956 could be entirely different from the vocabulary for 1976. This means, for example, that specific named entities could be driving the prediction accuracy. In order to test whether the feature space is specific to each year, we instead train classifiers that use a single feature space that is fit across the entire data set. This removes the importance of less common items like named entities because these entities are unlikely to occur often across this entire period. Thus, we now have two alternate versions of this model, each with slightly different features. And we want to determine whether this choice makes a difference.

In Figure 11, the blue line represents classification performance for our original system, and the red line represents performance when we use one set of features across the entire period. We see that the two results are quite close. From a visual inspection of the graph, we would think that there is no significant difference; but we need to be sure. Table 30 repeats the same metrics as Table 29: correlation, significance of correlation, and significance of the t-test. Here we see that the two sets of results are very significantly correlated and that there is no significant difference between them. This means that the choice of whether or not to refit the feature space for each congress has no impact on the performance of the classifier. And this, in turn, tells us that the prediction of party membership is not driven entirely by short-term entities like *Nixon* or *Watergate* or *Vietnam*, which would be relevant for only a short time.

This section has contextualized the performance of a classifier by adding baselines and comparing the performance of different systems. These methods allow us to determine whether our models are meaningful as a way to

Table 30 Relationship between classifiers with different feature spaces

Pearson Correlation	Correlation Significance	T-Test P-Value
0.866	0.001	0.641

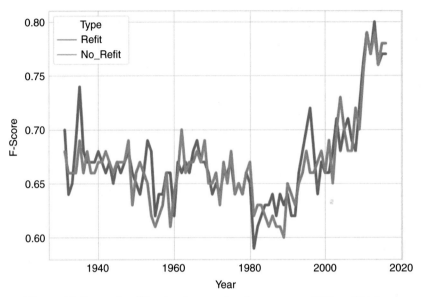

Figure 11 Party classification by year by feature type, 1931 to 2016, House only

systematically improve them. The lab for this section shows how to work with party prediction in more detail.[23]

4.2 Ensuring Validity Using Box Plots

In Section 2.8 we discussed implicit bias, which occurs when a model picks up on unrelated cues in a data set. This causes the model to make predictions that look accurate but are actually based on incorrect generalizations. This is called over-fitting. The basic idea is that the predictions of the model look accurate on a specific test set; but the model has been selected to fit that test set. In other words, if we had evaluated the model on a different set of examples, the prediction accuracy could be significantly lower.

Over-fitting is especially a problem when we are working with smaller data sets, like those that have been labeled by hand. If we only have a few hundred examples in the test set or if one of the classes is especially rare, then our performance is being evaluated on just a few examples. Let's say that we hand-label news articles by topic and there is a topic CORRUPTION that has only five examples. We put three examples in the training data and keep two examples in the testing data. This means that our classifier is being evaluated on just two examples of this class.

There are two techniques for dealing with this problem: **cross-validation** and **validation sets**. For a shallow classifier like logistic regression, which holds all the data in memory at once, we use **cross-validation**. The basic idea here is that we train and test many times, on different parts of the data. If we repeat our process five times, it is called 5-fold cross-validation; if we repeat the process ten times, it is called 10-fold cross-validation. In each case, we rotate what data is used for training and what data is used for testing until every sample has been used in the testing set once and only once. Thus, 10-fold cross-validation uses a 90/10 training/testing split. It is important to realize that cross-validation does not provide a single classifier, because we have actually trained and tested many different classifiers. But it does provide a robust understanding of the classifier's expected performance.

The second technique is called a **validation set**. This is what we use for a feed-forward network or other models that are trained incrementally on small batches. Because these models take longer to train, and because it is harder to estimate a stopping point, it would be impractical to train and test multiple feed-forward networks. Instead, the best practice is to divide the data into training, testing, and validation sets. Each training epoch is evaluated against the test set. This means that the classifier is exposed to the testing data, indirectly, many times throughout the training process. Thus, we also maintain an independent validation set that is only used at the end of the process to provide a final measure of model quality.

In this Element we have not focused on tuning or optimizing a model. But it turns out that every model, like logistic regression or a feed-forward network, has many parameters that need to be set. We must choose what values to use for each of these parameters and the parameter settings can have a significant impact on our final model. So, we often use significance testing to compare different models with various parameter settings as a way of finding the best options for a specific problem. Because there are so many choices, we would overuse our testing data if we evaluated every possibility.

For this reason, it is also best practice to use a development set. This means that we take a small bit of data to test the best model parameters. Then, we use a separate training/testing set to evaluate the best models. Subsequently, we evaluate the ultimate performance only once, using a reserved

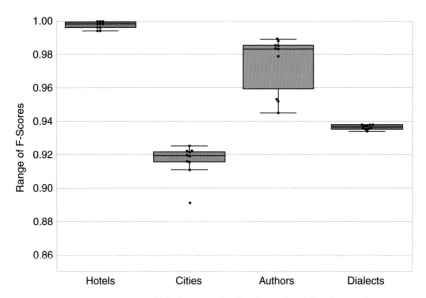

Figure 12 Cross-validation results for four classification tasks

validation set. These are all tools used to avoid over-fitting. Another way to think about these techniques is that they force us to replicate our own findings. The validation set or the application of cross-validation means that we as linguists have replicated our own studies before we submit them for peer review.

Let's see how this works in practice. In Section 2.1 we created a classifier to distinguish between dialects of English using constructions as features. And, in Section 2.2, we created a classifier to distinguish between different cities around the world using lexical features, including named entities. In Section 2.3 we made a model of authorship for nineteenth-century books using function word n-grams. Finally, in Section 2.5 we predicted the average rating of a hotel using sentiment features in hotel reviews. How robust are these results? Have we over-fitted in a way that inflates the performance of the classifiers? In Figure 12 we take a second look, reporting the cross-validation scores for each problem.

After doing this analysis, we see that all four experiments remain highly accurate during cross-validation, much higher than the majority baseline (not shown). Given the number of categories in these problems, the majority baseline is well below 0.50. This kind of replication is important to give us confidence in our results. The stable accuracy in all four cases shows that we have modeled the linguistic phenomena in question (dialects or author style, for example) rather than picking up on irrelevant cues and over-fitting the test set.

The lab for this section shows how to use these techniques to further evaluate our classification models to ensure validity.[24]

4.3 Unmasking Pseudonymous Authors Using Line Plots

Sometimes we need to visualize more than one model over time. For example, we have seen that we can use a text classifier to identify different authors using function word n-grams. When we work with books written by nineteenth-century authors, this model performs very well. But how robust is the classifier? How deep are these individual stylistic differences? Let's say that we have two writers, A and B. Writer A never starts a sentence with *And*. However, Writer B does so frequently. So, every text by Author A has zero sentences starting with *And*, but Author B has hundreds of sentences starting with *And*. We might have a classifier with perfect accuracy, but only because this one feature distinguishes between the two writers. We would not consider this model to be very meaningful: There is a lot more to stylistics than just this one feature.

To measure robustness, we use a technique called **unmasking** (Koppel, Schler, & Bonchek-Dokow, 2007), shown in Table 31. We train a logistic regression classifier to identify each author in the corpus. That means each feature in our vector, each function word n-gram, is getting a weight between −1 and 1. We can use the feature weights to find out what the most important features are. Unmasking works like this: We train and test the classifier many times. But, each time, we remove the most predictive features, one for each author. By the end of the unmasking process we have many different f-scores, each based on fewer predictive features.

If the model is trivial, the f-score will plummet once those few features have been removed. But, if the model is robust, the performance will decline very slowly. In other words, the more our model of authorship is distributed across

Table 31 Pseudo-code for the unmasking algorithm

Unmasking Algorithm	
	Repeat for *n* cycles:
Step 1	**Train** Logistic regression to classify books by author: The classifier provides feature weights for each author
Step 2	**Select** the most predictive features for each author: Remove those features from the vectors that represent each text

---

[24] Lab 4.2 –> https://doi.org/10.24433/CO.3402613.v1

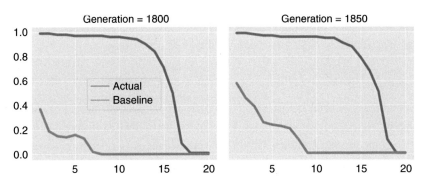

Figure 13 Unmasking performance for Authorship analysis

many different aspects of writing style, the more that model will remain accurate when a few salient features are removed. You will remember that we often
include L_2 normalization in the objective function, so that a model with extreme
feature weights is penalized for relying too much on a few predictive features.
The unmasking method visualizes this same property: How well are the model's
predictions distributed across all the features?

Let's take a look at what we find, shown in Figure 13. This is a facet grid
that shows the same experiment on two corpora: on the left with authors born
between 1800 and 1850, and then repeated on the right with authors born
between 1850 and 1900. We need a baseline to see if the results are meaningful,
so we also do authorship analysis in both contexts using just one author. We
choose one writer who produced many books in the corpus: Horatio Alger (who
wrote ninety-six books) and Jane Abbott (who wrote seventy-nine books). We
use these two prolific authors to simulate an imposter: a single writer who is
pretending to be multiple writers. Thus, the baseline task is to classify different
books that they wrote, using our same function word n-grams. In the one case
we distinguish between different individuals, and in the other case we try to
distinguish between writings from the same individual.

Figure 13 shows a line plot with the f-score over different cycles of feature
pruning. The x axis is the number of feature pruning cycles, twenty-five in total.
The classifier starts with about 10,000 function word n-grams and, as we move
to the right of the figure, this is pruned by removing one feature for each author
each cycle. That means we have removed up to the top 600 features for the 24
authors in the 1850 corpus. What happens to performance? The y axis is the
prediction accuracy, measured using the f-score. This means that the higher the
line, the better the classifier works.

And we see that, for the real authorship task, the model is quite robust. The
performance remains strong until between cycles 12 and 15, then plummets

rather quickly. That is exactly what we expect to see, because the model of writing style is based on many different grammatical forms. So getting rid of a few isolated features does not reduce performance, until we have removed so many features that the classifier is unable to contextualize the less common features. In other words, we have identified the depth of this classifier, the point where the performance drops off.

But, for the baseline task, we start off with a much lower f-score because it is difficult to predict individual books when they were all written by the same person. And then we see a rather sharp decline: Every time we remove a few features, the f-score goes down dramatically. This sharp decline is exactly what we expect when the model is not robust. In other words, this validation method allows us to see how quickly the performance drops; and, in both cases here, the difference between real authorship and pretend authorship is quite clear.

The point of this section has been to show how line plots and facet grids can be used to visualize models over time, in this case over cycles of feature pruning. This method measures the degree to which a classifier depends on only a few features. This is another way to validate a model, adding another piece of evidence that a model is making meaningful predictions. In the lab for this section we use the *text_analytics* package to carry out the unmasking analysis.[25]

4.4 Comparing Word Embeddings Using Heat Maps

Because of variation from dialects and registers, we expect that large corpora will contain diverging patterns. For example, we have worked with texts from 1931 to 2016 from both lead paragraphs in *The New York Times* and speeches in the US congress. These are different registers and they potentially represent different populations of speakers as well. As a result, we do not expect that the corpora will contain the same linguistic patterns. Following from that, we do not expect that the word embeddings from both corpora will provide exactly the same semantic relationships.

We previously used distance measures like cosine and Euclidean distance to compare individual words and individual documents. Another way to visualize the relationship between words, as in Figure 14, is to reduce our high-dimensional word embeddings to two dimensions (x and y) using principal components analysis or PCA. This is a common method that allows us to create a scatterplot to show how words are distributed around this reduced semantic space. But, from a linguistic perspective, how do we know that a particular

---

[25] Lab 4.3 –> https://doi.org/10.24433/CO.3402613.v1

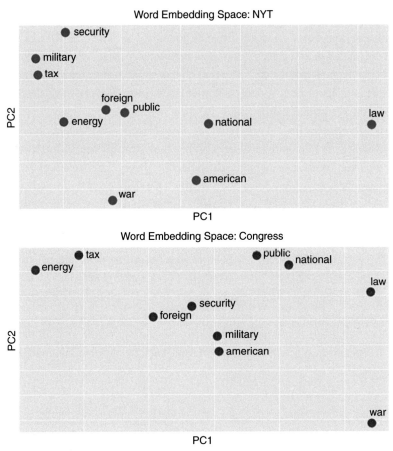

Figure 14 Visualizing word embeddings from news articles and speeches

configuration is good or bad? As we see in the labs, it is quite difficult to compare multiple different corpora using this method while maintaining our goal of reproducibility and falsifiability.

Let's contrast the same set of words in both of these corpora. The corpora represent formal registers from the same period of American history. And yet we see some striking differences. In the congressional corpus, *military* and *american* are quite close; but in the news corpus they are quite distant. On the other hand, in the news corpus the words *energy* and *public* are quite close and, thus, quite similar. But in the congressional corpus these words are quite distant. In fact, *energy* is nearest to *tax*. The point here is that this kind of visualization seems like it is telling us about vector semantics. But the visualization is very different across these two corpora (the labs consider several more as well) and we only have our intuitions to tell us how different the overall embeddings actually are. So let's find a more reproducible method.

Instead we will use the **Jaccard similarity** to measure the overlap of two sets of embeddings. This is a measure of set overlap: How similar are two independent sets of words? We choose 200 words that are frequent in 5 different corpora: news articles, congressional speeches, tweets and web pages, nineteenth-century books, and hotel reviews. For each word, we collect the five most similar words according to the embeddings, as calculated using cosine similarity. This gives us 200 sets of 5 words for each corpus.

$$J(A,B) = \frac{|A \cap B|}{|A \cup B|} \tag{4.1}$$

The Jaccard similarity, shown above as J, is the ratio of the intersection of the two sets to the union of the two sets. In this case, the two sets A and B are the top five most similar words for each target word in each set of embeddings. When this value is low, there is little overlap between the embeddings in terms of their predicted most similar words. A low overlap could result from different vocabularies: For instance, if a word does not occur in the congressional speeches corpus, it will never be a member of the set of most similar words. Or it could result from the embeddings finding different patterns of similarity, in essence producing a different vector space for describing the same words.

We visualize the relationship between embeddings from the five corpora in Figure 15. The most similar embeddings are news articles and congressional speeches (both representing the same time period). The least similar are nineteenth-century books and hotel reviews. This reflects our expectation that differences in register and population (here caused by time) will produce different linguistic patterns. Because word embeddings are based on

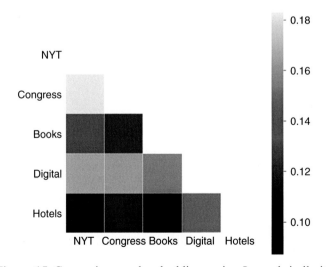

Figure 15 Comparing word embeddings using Jaccard similarity

patterns observed in a corpus, these variations between corpora have a significant impact on the final representations. Such differences do not imply that the embeddings do not carry meaningful information. But they do imply that there is not a single vector space for a language, and certainly not a single vector space for all human languages.

The basic finding here is that distributional representations of word meaning can vary significantly across corpora. One reason for this variation is variation in the corpora themselves. Another reason, mentioned above, is that word2vec approximates methods that are based on a matrix of association values. This approximation is more efficient but less stable. This relatively low level of agreement between embeddings is perfectly acceptable unless we want to interpret the embeddings as a universal meaning representation that somehow generalizes beyond the corpus that it describes. We must be careful about the generalizations that we draw about a language or all languages when using techniques like this. The lab for this section takes a deeper look at comparing word embeddings across these five sets of corpora.[26]

4.5 Following Linguistic Diversity using Choropleth Maps

In this section we explore the use of choropleth maps, drawing on data from tweets and web pages. What can these sources of language data tell us about the linguistic diversity of particular countries? This is another application of corpus analysis to a nonlinguistic question, or at least a question that falls outside of traditional linguistic analysis. The goal is to measure a proxy or indicator, using language data, for a socioeconomic quantity. First, we need to develop a text-based measure to capture the language that each sample represents. Second, we need to visualize the distribution of languages given a set of predicted language labels. In order to visualize this information we will use a map instead of a traditional figure.

First, we rely on a classifier to assign language labels to individual tweets and web pages in order to know exactly what languages we are observing. We use a feed-forward network for this purpose, a model that identifies a total of 464 languages (Dunn, 2020). This model is rather similar to what we have seen in Section 2: using frequency vectors for character n-grams within a text classifier. But here the goal is to predict language labels rather than to predict a dialect or a part of speech.[27]

Given a classifier for predicting the language of each sample, we map languages by country using tweets (a total of 17 billion words) and web pages

---

[26] Lab 4.4 –> https://doi.org/10.24433/CO.3402613.v1
[27] https://github.com/jonathandunn/idNet

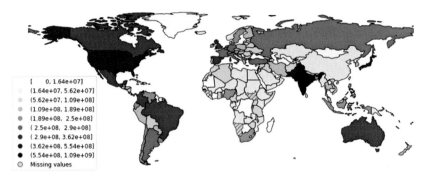

Figure 16 Number of words per country, corpus of tweets

(a total of 400 billion words). This gives us an estimate of the distribution of languages over countries from a digital perspective. The map in Figure 16 shows the distribution of the corpus of tweets by number of words per country. Clearly, some parts of the world are better represented than others. For example, North America and Western Europe have more data than most of Africa and Southeast Asia. This map is useful on its own, in the sense that current computational methods rely on corpora like this which are skewed toward some parts of the world's population.

The question, then, is to find a single measure for how many different languages are being used in a particular country, without being specific as to which languages those are. There is a lot of data per country, so we cannot simply count the number of languages which appear. Instead, we use the Herfindahl–Hirschman Index or HHI (Dunn, Coupe, & Adams, 2020). As shown below, this is the sum of the square of the share of each language. For example, if English accounts for 60 percent of the data from a country, Spanish accounts for 30 percent, and French accounts for 10 percent, that gives us: $(0.6)^2 + (0.3)^2 + (0.1)^2 = 0.36 + 0.09 + 0.01 = 0.46$. Higher values indicate a larger monopoly, in which a few languages account for much of the digital data. This is calculated for each language (L_n) in a country, although the influence of very infrequent languages becomes very small. This is helpful given the possibility of a small number of incorrect labels in the data set.

$$HHI = [Share(L_1)^2 + Share(L_2)^2 + Share(L_3)^2 \ldots Share(L_n)^2] \qquad (4.2)$$

We see linguistic diversity by country for tweets in Figure 17. In digital contexts, English is more pervasive than in nondigital contexts. Thus, countries which are more monolingual in non-English languages (like France or Spain) will have lower HHI values, appearing more diverse because there is a significant presence of English in this digital context. The most monolingual countries are the USA, Brazil, and Argentina. The most multilingual countries are India

[0.144, 0.190]
(0.190, 0.258]
(0.258, 0.324]
(0.324, 0.409]
(0.409, 0.525]
(0.525, 0.644]
(0.644, 0.747]
(0.747, 0.840]
(0.840, 0.931]
Missing values

Figure 17 Linguistic diversity (HHI) by country, tweet corpus

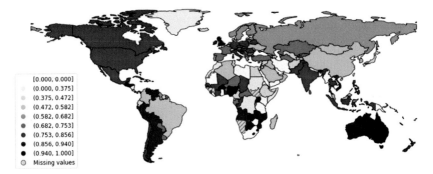

[0.000, 0.000]
(0.000, 0.375]
(0.375, 0.472]
(0.472, 0.582]
(0.582, 0.682]
(0.682, 0.753]
(0.753, 0.856]
(0.856, 0.940]
(0.940, 1.000]
Missing values

Figure 18 Linguistic diversity (HHI) by country, web corpus

and a large number of the countries in South Asia, as well as most countries in Africa. Because the HHI looks at the relative share of languages in each country, it is not influenced by variations in the size of the corpus for each country.

The corpus of tweets provides one source of observations, but of course a platform like this is inconsistent because it competes with different platforms across different countries. In Figure 18 we contrast this with the corpus drawn from web data. We see the same general trends; here, however, Brazil is much more multilingual while India is more monolingual. While either source of data is somewhat biased, it is often possible to triangulate across different sources like this to correct that bias (Dunn, 2021).

The point of this section has been that we can use a text classifier to predict the language for samples from digital corpora. These labels, when combined with metadata for space and time, can provide a socioeconomic measure of linguistic diversity, at least for digital contexts. Because this kind of information is likely to be structured geographically, we visualize it using maps. The lab for this section shows in more detail how to map linguistic phenomena.[28]

---

[28] Lab 4.5 –> https://doi.org/10.24433/CO.3402613.v1

4.6 Ethics: Equal Access

We know that speakers of different languages from different geographic areas do not have the same degree of access to digital technologies. We have seen throughout this Element that we can learn a great deal about language and about populations using computational linguistic analysis. But in order for this analysis to be possible, we need to have large amounts of digital data. Unfortunately, most languages simply do not have corpora of this size available. And that means the people who speak those languages are not represented by the increasingly important computational models that depend on large corpora.

Figure 19 shows the countries of the world by their representation in the *Corpus of Global Language Use* (Dunn, 2020). Hosted at earthLings.io,[29] this is one of the largest corpora in the world. Here we are looking at the amount of data per country in number of words. There are many factors involved in the production of digital data, but the main ones are (i) population, (ii) internet access, and (iii) GDP. Wealthy countries produce more language data per person in digital contexts (Dunn & Adams, 2019).

Traditional methods of linguistic analysis are not impacted by this kind of bias in the production of digital data, although they continue to show a strong bias toward languages from wealthy Western countries. But the methods that we have learned about in this Element, because they take advantage of large corpora, are particularly subject to population-based bias. This is a perverse side effect of taking advantage of large-scale computational analysis: It is only possible on well-represented majority languages.

Only around fifty languages have public corpora available that can support the kinds of methods we have covered in this Element. All other languages are, in effect, low-resource languages. Table 32 shows the languages in the

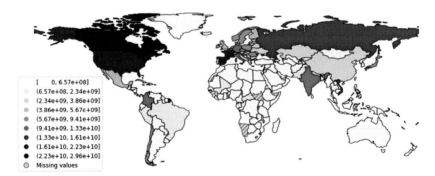

Figure 19 Corpus size by country, *Corpus of Global Language Use*

---

[29] https://www.earthLings.io

Table 32 Similarity of balanced and unbalanced word embeddings

Code	Language	Jaccard	Code	Language	Jaccard
ara	Arabic	0.1318	bul	Bulgarian	0.1713
cat	Catalan	0.1525	ces	Czech	0.2005
dan	Danish	0.1596	deu	German	0.2140
ell	Greek	0.1131	eng	Eng. (Inner)	0.1873
eng	Engl. (Outer)	0.2139	eng	Eng. (Expand)	0.2169
est	Estonian	0.1883	fas	Farsi	0.2092
fin	Finnish	0.2020	fra	French	0.1670
gle	Irish	0.0880	hin	Hindi	0.0285
hun	Hungarian	0.2257	ind	Indonesian	0.2252
ita	Italian	0.1726	jpn	Japanese	0.0962
kaz	Kazakh	0.1442	kor	Korean	0.0717
lav	Latvian	0.1687	nld	Dutch	0.2200
pol	Polish	0.1835	por	Portuguese	0.1876
ron	Romanian	0.1902	rus	Russian	0.1508
slk	Slovak	0.1684	slv	Slovenian	0.1602
spa	Spanish	0.1908	swe	Swedish	0.1733
tur	Turkish	0.1674	ukr	Ukrainian	0.1714
vie	Vietnamese	0.0254	zho	Chinese	0.0447

GeoWAC project (Dunn & Adams, 2020). This project has the goal of making gigaword corpora (containing at least a billion words) available in as many languages as possible, while accurately sampling the users of each language. In other words, the GeoWAC corpus of English includes samples from Nigeria and New Zealand instead of just the USA and UK. On the one hand, projects like this make it possible for computational linguistic analysis to provide equal access for diverse populations. But, on the other hand, this is still only a first attempt to mitigate this perverse side effect of computational methods.

Does it make a difference for a language like English to be represented by only American speakers or a language like Spanish by only European speakers? Although the population of users of these languages are spread around the world, traditional corpora are largely restricted to so-called *inner-circle* varieties. The table shows the agreement between word embeddings trained on geographically biased data (drawn exclusively from inner-circle countries) and unbiased data (drawn from many countries using population-based sampling). There is a fairly low agreement overall using the same Jaccard similarity method we saw in Section 4.4.

We are comparing embeddings from two sets of gigaword corpora: one that is balanced to avoid population-bias and one that is not balanced. The wide variation that we observe means that our vector semantics for each language actually represents only a narrow population of users of that language, ignoring much of the world. If our goal is to model the vector semantics of American English, this is not a problem. But as soon as we try to generalize to the vector semantics of English or to a language-universal semantics, these findings become quite problematic.

The purpose of this section is not to discredit the endeavour of computational linguistic analysis. After all, this remains a powerful tool for undertaking linguistic analysis on a large scale. But it is important that we do not overlook the weaknesses that remain, both ethical and theoretical. Once we have identified those problems (implicit bias, discrimination, lack of equal access), we can work to correct them. That is exactly the goal of projects like GeoWAC.

5 Conclusions

This Element has shown how computational methods from natural language processing can expand and scale up corpus linguistics by helping us to solve a wide range of categorization and comparison problems. At the same time, we have taken a closer look at the theoretical and ethical issues that arise when we use these computational methods. It is important that we consider the technical aspects, the linguistic aspects, and the ethical aspects together.

For categorization problems, we have seen how we can convert the linguistic signal into a vector representation that highlights semantics (content), pragmatics (sentiment), style (syntactic choices across a document), and context (local syntactic relationships). Once we have converted the corpus data into a shared vector space, we can make highly accurate predictions about authorship and dialect membership, about parts of speech, about lexical content, and about positive or negative sentiment. This wide range of applications is made possible by a powerful model, a text classifier.

At the same time, many linguistic questions do not involve discrete categories. We have seen how comparison problems require a continuous measure of similarity. This allows us to study relationships between pairs of items, like words or documents. At the level of corpora, we have looked at relationships between registers. At the level of documents, we have looked at relationships based on syntactic, semantic, and pragmatic features. At the level of words, we have looked at relationships in distribution using both association measures and word embeddings. And, finally, we have seen how we can construct a network of pairwise relationships by using clustering algorithms to put the most similar pairs into a single categorical group.

Is there always a clear distinction between categorization and comparison problems? It turns out that there is a good deal of interaction between these two classes of methods. We have seen that word embeddings are a method of approximating an association matrix using logistic regression. The basic idea is to train a classifier to predict which words occur together, a task we are not directly focused on, in order to extract feature weights that work well for other tasks. A very popular method is to then use word embeddings as the first layer in a neural network. In other words, we first train an unsupervised model on a very large corpus and then we take that unsupervised model as a starting point for a supervised categorization task.

How does this work? The details are shown in the *text_analytics* package in the function called *mlp_embeddings*. We essentially combine a word embedding (Section 3.5) with a positional vector (Section 2.4). We then represent each document using concatenated word embeddings. So, imagine the first word in the document is *cats* and the next words are *sit* and *on* and *mats*. We take the 100-dimensional embedding for *cats* and add the 100-dimensional embedding for *sit* and add the 100-dimensional embedding for *on*, and so on.

This creates a vector of positionally encoded word embeddings. For our bag-of-words vectors, we often use 10,000 or more features to describe a document. And, in this case, the representation for a 100-word document again contains a vector of 10,000 features (100 words * 100 dimensions for each word). A vector like this is given to a feed-forward neural network, which is able to slowly update those embeddings until they perform well on a specific classification task.

The point here is that we have a lot of tools available for computational linguistic analysis. And, importantly, we can mix and match those tools. We often reuse a few important techniques, like co-occurrence probabilities or feature weights, over and over again in different contexts.

The interactive code notebooks have shown how to reproduce all of the examples in this Element. You can go further into the details by using the stand-alone Python package[30] that we used to support those notebooks. This package shows how to implement all of these methods using best practices. It is a good place to start for those intending to implement these methods on their own corpora for analysis in their own computational environment.

---

[30] https://github.com/jonathandunn/text_analytics

References

Biber, D. (2012). Register as a Predictor of Linguistic Variation. *Corpus Linguistics and Linguistic Theory, 8*(1), 9–37.

Church, K., & Hanks, P. (1990). Word Association Norms, Mutual Information, and Lexicography. *Computational Linguistics, 16*(1), 22–29.

Diermeier, D., Godbout, J., Yu, B., & Kaufmann, S. (2011). Language and Ideology in Congress. *British Journal of Political Science, 42*(1), 31–55.

Dunn, J. (2013a). Evaluating the Premises and Results of Four Metaphor Identification Systems. In A. Gelbukh (ed.), *Proceedings of the Conference on Intelligent Text Processing and Computational Linguistics, vol. 1* (pp. 471–486). Heidelberg: Springer.

Dunn, J. (2013). How Linguistic Structure Influences and Helps to Predict Metaphoric Meaning. *Cognitive Linguistics, 24*(1), 33–66.

Dunn, J. (2014). Measuring Metaphoricity. In K. Toutanova & H. Wu (eds.), *Proceedings of the Annual Meeting of the Association for Computational Linguistics* (pp. 745–751). Stroudsburg, PA: Association for Computational Linguistics.

Dunn, J. (2015). Modeling Abstractness and Metaphoricity. *Metaphor & Symbol, 30,* 259–289.

Dunn, J. (2017). Computational Learning of Construction Grammars. *Language & Cognition, 9*(2), 254–292.

Dunn, J. (2018a). Finding Variants for Construction-Based Dialectometry: A Corpus-Based Approach to Regional CxGs. *Cognitive Linguistics, 29*(2), 275–311.

Dunn, J. (2018b). Modeling the Complexity and Descriptive Adequacy of Construction Grammars. In G. Jarosz, B. O'Connor, & J. Pater (eds.), *Proceedings of the Society for Computation in Linguistics* (pp. 81–90). Stroudsburg, PA: Association for Computational Linguistics.

Dunn, J. (2018c). Multi-Unit Directional Measures of Association Moving Beyond Pairs of Words. *International Journal of Corpus Linguistics, 23*(2), 183–215.

Dunn, J. (2019a). Frequency vs. Association for Constraint Selection in Usage-Based Construction Grammar. In E. Chersoni, C. Jacobs, A. Lenci, T. Linzen, L. Prévot, & E. Santus (eds.), *Proceedings of the Workshop on Cognitive Modeling and Computational Linguistics* (pp. 117–128). Stroudsburg, PA: Association: for Computational Linguistics.

Dunn, J. (2019b). Global Syntactic Variation in Seven Languages: Towards a Computational Dialectology. *Frontiers in Artificial Intelligence,* Collection on Computational Sociolinguistics, 2. DOI: https://doi.org/10.3389/frai.2019.00015.

Dunn, J. (2019c). Modeling Global Syntactic Variation in English Using Dialect Classification. In M. Zampieri, P. Nakov, S. Malmasi, N. Ljubešić, J. Tiedemann, & A. Ali (eds.), *Proceedings of NAACL 2019 Sixth Workshop on NLP for Similar Languages, Varieties and Dialects* (pp. 42–53). Stroudsburg, PA: Association for Computational Linguistics.

Dunn, J. (2020). Mapping Languages: The Corpus of Global Language Use. *Language Resources and Evaluation, 54,* 999–1018. DOI: https://doi.org/10.1007/s10579-020-09489-2.

Dunn, J. (2021). Representations of Language Varieties Are Reliable Given Corpus Similarity Measures. In M. Zampieri, P. Nakov, N. Ljubešić, J. Tiedemann, Y. Scherrer, & T. Jahuiainen (Eds.), *Proceedings of the Eighth Workshop on NLP for Similar Languages, Varieties, and Dialects* (pp. 28–38). Stroudsburg, PA: Association for Computational Linguistics.

Dunn, J., & Adams, B. (2019). Mapping Languages and Demographics with Georeferenced Corpora. In B. Adams, M. de Roiste, M. Gahegan, C. Hulbe, D. O'Sullivan, K. Sila-Nowicka, P. Whigham, & M. Wilson (eds.), *Proceedings of Geocomputation 2019* (16 pp.). Auckland: N.p.

Dunn, J., & Adams, B. (2020, May). Geographically-Balanced Gigaword Corpora for 50 Language Varieties. In N. Calzolari, F. Béchet, P. Blache, K. Choukri, C. Cieri, T. Declerck, S. Goggi, H. Isahara, B. Maegaard, J. Mariani, H. Mazo, A. Moreno, J. Odijk, & S. Piperidis (eds.), *Proceedings of the 12th Language Resources and Evaluation Conference* (pp. 2528–2536). Marseilles, European Language Resources Association.

Dunn, J., Argamon, S., Rasooli, A., & Kumar, G. (2016). Profile-Based Authorship Analysis. *Literary and Linguistic Computing, 31*(4), 689–710.

Dunn, J., Coupe, T., & Adams, B. (2020, Nov.). Measuring Linguistic Diversity During COVID-19. In D. Bamman, D. Hovy, D. Jurgens, B. O'Connor, & S. Volkova (eds.), *Proceedings of the Fourth Workshop on Natural Language Processing and Computational Social Science* (pp. 1–10). Online: Association for Computational Linguistics.

Dunn, J., & Nini, A. (2021). Production vs Perception: The Role of Individuality in Usage-Based Grammar Induction. In E. Chersoni, N. Hollenstein, C. Jacobs, Y. Oseki, L. Prévot, & E. Santus (Eds.), *Proceedings of the Workshop on Cognitive Modeling and Computational Linguistics* (pp. 149–159). Stroudsburg, PA: Association for Computational Linguistics.

Dunn, J., & Tayyar Madabushi, H. (2021). Learned Construction Grammars Converge Across Registers Given Increased Exposure. In A. Bisazza &

O. Abend (Eds.), *Proceedings of the Conference on Computational Natural Language Learning* (pp. 471–486). Stroudsburg, PA: Association for Computational Linguistics.

Ellis, N. (2007). Language Acquisition as Rational Contingency Learning. *Applied Linguistics, 27*(1), 1–24.

Francis, W., & Kucera, H. (1967). *Computational Analysis of Present-Day American English.* Providence, RI: Brown University Press.

Gentzkow, M., Shapiro, J., & Taddy, M. (2018). *Congressional Record for the 43rd–114th Congresses: Parsed Speeches and Phrase Counts* (Tech. Rep.). Palo Alto, CA: Stanford Libraries. https://data.stanford.edu/congress_text

Gerlach, M., & Font-Clos, F. (2020). A Standardized Project Gutenberg Corpus for Statistical Analysis of Natural Language and Quantitative Linguistics. *Entropy, 22*(1), 126. DOI: https://doi.org/10.3390/e22010126

Goldberg, Y. (2017). *Neural Network Methods in Natural Language Processing.* Williston, VT: Morgan & Claypool Publishers.

Gries, S. T. (2013). 50-Something Years of Work on Collocations: What Is or Should Be Next. *International Journal of Corpus Linguistics, 18*(1), 137–165.

Hellrich, J., Kampe, B., & Hahn, U. (2019). The Influence of Down-Sampling Strategies on SVD Word Embedding Stability. In A. Rogers, A. Drozd, A. Rumshisky, & Y. Goldberg (Eds.), *Proceedings of the 3rd Workshop on Evaluating Vector Space Representations for NLP* (pp. 18–26). Stroudburg, PA: Association for Computational Linguistics.

Kilgarriff, A. (2001). Comparing Corpora. *International Journal of Corpus Linguistics, 6*(1), 97–133.

Koppel, M., Schler, J., & Bonchek-Dokow, E. (2007). Measuring Differentiability: Unmasking Pseudonymous Authors. *Journal of Machine Learning Research, 8,* 1261–1276.

Landauer, T., Foltz, P., & Laham, D. (1998). Introduction to Latent Semantic Analysis. *Discourse Processes, 25*(2–3), 259–284.

Levy, O., Goldberg, Y., & Dagan, I. (2015, May). Improving Distributional Similarity with Lessons Learned from Word Embeddings. *Transactions of the Association for Computational Linguistics, 3,* 211–225.

Li, J. (2012). *Hotel Reviews Dataset* (Tech. Rep.). Carnegie Mellon University. www.cs.cmu.edu/~jiweil/html/hotel-review.html

McKenzie, G., & Adams, B. (2018). A Data-Driven Approach to Exploring Similarities of Tourist Attractions through Online Reviews. *Journal of Location Based Services, 12*(2), 94–118.

Mikolov, T., Sutskever, I., Chen, K., Corrado, G., & Dean, J. (2013). Distributed Representations of Words and Phrases and Their Compositionality. In

C. J. C. Burges, L. Bottou, M. Welling, Z. Ghahramani, & K. Q. Weinberger (Eds.), *Proceedings of the 26th International Conference on Neural Information Processing Systems–Volume 2* (pp. 3111–3119). Red Hook, NY: Curran Associates Inc.

Mueller, A., Nicolai, G., Petrou-Zeniou, P., Talmina, N., & Linzen, T. (2020). Cross-Linguistic Syntactic Evaluation of Word Prediction Models. In D. Jurafsky, J. Chai, N. Schluter, & J. Tetreault (Eds.), *Proceedings of the 58th Annual Meeting of the Association for Computational Linguistics* (pp. 5523–5539). Stroudsburg, PA: Association for Computational Linguistics.

Parsons, A. (2019). *NY Times Article Lead Paragraphs 1851–2017* (Tech. Rep.). Kaggle. https://www.kaggle.com/parsonsandrew1/nytimes-article-lead-paragraphs-18512017

Pennebaker, J. (2011). *The Secret Life of Pronouns: What Our Words Say About Us.* New York: Bloomsbury Publishing.

Pennington, J., Socher, R., & Manning, C. (2014). GloVe: Global Vectors for Word Representation. In A. Moschitti, B. Pang, & W. Daelemans (eds.), *Empirical Methods in Natural Language Processing (EMNLP)* (pp. 1532–1543). Stroudsburg, PA: Association for Computational Linguistics.

Petrov, S., Das, D., & McDonald, R. (2012). A Universal Part-of-Speech Tagset. In N. Calzolari, K. Choukri, T. Declerck, M. Uğur Doğan, B. Maegaard, J. Mariani, A. Moreno, J. Odijk, & S. Piperidis (eds.), *Proceedings of the Eighth Conference on Language Resources and Evaluation* (pp. 2089–2096). Paris: European Language Resources Association.

Taylor, J. (2004). *Linguistic Categorization* (3rded.). Oxford: Oxford University Press.

Wang, H., Lu, Y., & Zhai, C. (2011). Latent Aspect Rating Analysis Without Aspect Keyword Supervision. In *Proceedings of the 17th ACM SIGKDD Conference on Knowledge Discovery and Data Mining* (pp. 618–626). New York: Association for Computing Machinery.

Zeman, D. et al. (2021). *Universal Dependencies 2.8.1* (Tech. Rep.). LINDAT/CLARIAH-CZ Digital Library at the Institute of Formal and Applied Linguistics (ÚFAL), Faculty of Mathematics and Physics, Charles University. http://hdl.handle.net/11234/1-3687

Zhao, J., Zhou, Y., Li, Z., Wang, W., & Chang, K.-W. (2018, October–November). Learning Gender-Neutral Word Embeddings. In E. Riloff, D. Chiang, J. Hockenmaier, & J. Tsujii (eds.), *Proceedings of the 2018 Conference on Empirical Methods in Natural Language Processing* (pp. 4847–4853). Brussels: Association for Computational Linguistics.

Zuboff, S. (2019). *The Age of Surveillance Capitalism: The Fight for a Human Future at the New Frontier of Power.* New York: PublicAffairs.

Acknowledgments

This Element has benefited tremendously from contributions from colleagues at the University of Canterbury. The case-study approach would not have been possible without previous collaborations with Jeanette King, Tom Coupé, and Girish Prayag. The presentation would have been much more complicated without the coaching of Kaushik Kumar, Michael Philpott, and Rob Stowell. The integration of digital resources like code notebooks has been improved by feedback from Carmen Weaver and Richard Davies. The *text_analytics* package has benefited greatly from generalizations added by Damian Sastre. The exercises in corpus similarity would not have been possible without the work of Haipeng Li.

Data Availability Statement

The Python code and corpus data accompanying this Element can be run interactively online via Code Ocean. The link can be found below:

https://doi.org/10.24433/CO.3402613.v1

Cambridge Elements ⊒

Corpus Linguistics

Susan Hunston
University of Birmingham

Professor of English Language at the University of Birmingham, UK. She has been involved in Corpus Linguistics for many years and has written extensively on corpora, discourse, and the lexis-grammar interface. She is probably best known as the author of Corpora in Applied Linguistics (2002, Cambridge University Press). Susan is currently co-editor, with Carol Chapelle, of the Cambridge Applied Linguistics series.

Advisory Board
Professor Paul Baker, *Lancaster University*
Professor Jesse Egbert, *Northern Arizona University*
Professor Gaetanelle Gilquin, *Université Catholique de Louvain*

About the Series
Corpus Linguistics has grown to become part of the mainstream of Linguistics and Applied Linguistics, as well as being used as an adjunct to other forms of discourse analysis in a variety of fields. It continues to become increasingly complex, both in terms of the methods it uses and in relation to the theoretical concepts it engages with. The Cambridge Elements in Corpus Linguistics series has been designed to meet the needs of both students and researchers who need to keep up with this changing field. The series includes introductions to the main topic areas by experts in the field as well as accounts of the latest ideas and developments by leading researchers.

Cambridge Elements ≡

Corpus Linguistics

Printed in the United States
by Baker & Taylor Publisher Services